D1094264

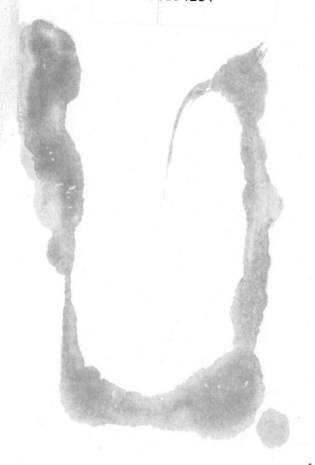

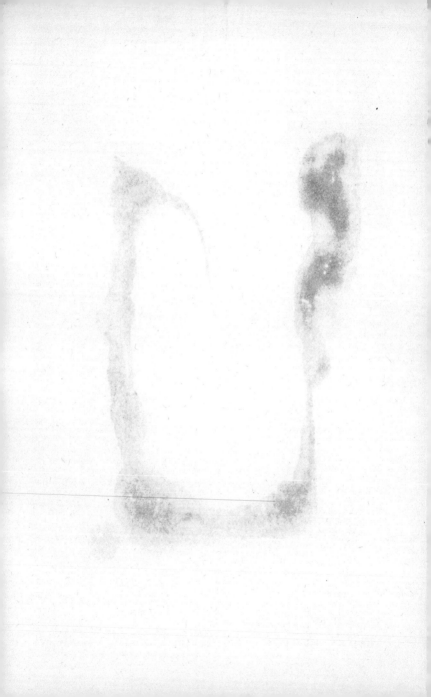

'TAKE AND READ'

also by E. H. Robertson

MAN'S ESTIMATE OF MAN

'Take and Read'

A GUIDE TO GROUP BIBLE STUDY

by

E. H. ROBERTSON

WITHDRAWN

John Knox Press

RICHMOND VIRGINIA

Published simultaneously in Great Britain by
SCM Press Ltd, London and in the United
States of America by John Knox Press,
Richmond, Virginia

Copyright © 1961 SCM Press Ltd

Library of Congress Catalog Card Number:
61-6688

PRINTED IN GREAT BRITAIN

CONTENTS

'Suddenly, I heard the voice of a child coming from the neighbouring house, chanting over and over again, "Take and read, take and read" . . . I snatched up the apostle's book, opened it, and in silence read.'

Augustine, *Confessions*, VIII, XII, 29.

PREFACE

This book is intended to help those who wish to undertake effective Bible study, whether as individuals or as groups. It will be particularly valuable, I hope, to those who are to meet in small groups seeking to discover what the Word of God has to say to them.

The material for this book has been collected mostly in the course of my duties as Study Secretary of the United Bible Societies, when I was assigned the task of discovering what was really happening to the Bible in the churches. It was a task involving a survey of Bible use in many different countries, but the material from Europe has been predominant in this book. It was in Europe that I first began the study. It was also part of these studies to assess the material gathered and to discover what was really effective Bible use, particularly that use which could be recommended to other countries. Many of the recommendations made in this book are made as the result of sifting material found in Europe and examining the British and American scenes to discover what lessons the churches of the English-speaking world might learn from the churches of Europe. There are, of course, many things that the churches of Europe could learn from the churches of the English-speaking world, but this book is not about that.

In collecting this material, and in its final arrangement in book form, I am indebted to the valuable help of my Assistant, Miss Lesley Walmsley, who was particularly helpful in compiling the material for the sample Bible study on Hosea 2, described in Chapter 3. My thanks are also due to the many churches in Europe who have patiently explained to me their methods of Bible use, and to those who have allowed me to sit in on their discussions. Biblical quotations are from the Revised Standard Version unless otherwise stated.

E. H. ROBERTSON.

I

REALLY EFFECTIVE BIBLE STUDY

WHAT is really effective Bible study? It can best be defined as that study of the Bible which enables a man to go out and live fully in his world. So long as a culture is pursuing the even tenor of its ways there is no real difficulty in a man living by tradition and studying his Bible without that study having any drastic effect upon the way in which he lives. In such peaceful periods, two types of Bible study grow up which are really ineffective and, if they are carried over into a stormy period of history like our own, they will become dangerously ineffective. The two methods are those of the pietist and the liberal. Not all who can be described by these names are guilty of the worst extremes of these two methods of Bible study, but the tendency is there, and there are plenty of examples of the worst extremes in practice.

THE PIETIST

The way of the pietist is to study the Bible as belonging to another world. He will thereby build for himself a biblical world which he enjoys and in which he lives with his brethren apart from the real world outside. It will be an escape for him to study his Bible. There have been times when this method of Bible study has had its value. When

9

the world is toppling about him a man may well wish to hide himself and to hold on to his personal faith. But such Bible study will often lead him to be ineffective in his world. The best example of this in modern times can be found among some of the pietistic sects of Germany. During the Nazi period they escaped into their Bible study and took no responsible action against the evils of their society.

THE LIBERAL

The way of the liberal is a study of the Bible which may lead to the discovery of certain abiding truths but which will on the whole neglect the authoritative message of the Bible. It is all too often a finding in the Bible of illustrations for truths which have been arrived at by the use of reason. The Bible then becomes simply a book of illustrations: those which are good are used, those which are not are neglected. The supremacy of reason over the Bible sometimes leads to an analysis of the books of the Bible to such an extent that they have lost their life. They are dissected as dead documents. In academic study a man may become so fascinated by the game of pulling the Bible to pieces that he has no chance of ever hearing its message. A good example of this in modern times is seen in the liberals of Germany under the Nazis. They had already been severely weakened by the attacks of Karl Barth upon their theology, and they fell an easy prey to Nazism. There are times when the liberal approach is necessary, and it has given to us a sound text of the Bible and a whole library of reliable commentaries. The work of the liberals must not be underestimated, for it has been of supreme worth in the development of our understanding of the Bible. In times of peace the liberals have their work to do. In stormy days like our own there is a need for Bible study which is more intensely personal than anything the liberals could conceive. To study the Bible academically today may be a contribution to culture, but it is not effective Bible study.

THE JOINING OF THE STREAMS

Both the examples of ineffective Bible study have been taken from Germany because in the history of the German churches both can be seen most clearly. For one hundred and fifty years the *Gemeinschaft* movements have been a strength to the piety of the German churches. Neither can anyone deny that the Germans have taken a lead in biblical scholarship. Yet these two streams never blended until recent years. They were almost forced together by the influence of the Nazi regime. Not all would join with the other stream, and as the examples so far quoted illustrate, the *Gemeinschaft* movements as a whole went underground and the liberal movement collapsed. But those who saw the need of the hour emerged strengthened to supply a new stream in Bible study to enrich the life of Germany.

KARL BARTH

There was a theological movement in Germany which coincided in time with the rise of the Nazi Party. It was in some ways strengthened by it, not because it approved of the Party but because it was the only effective weapon against it. This movement has usually been called Barthian, because one of the main inspirations of the movement was the dauntless figure of the theologian, Karl Barth. His theology gave to many scholars a new basis for believing in the Bible. They saw that they need not accept the narrow views of the *Gemeinschaft* movements if they were to believe that the Bible was the Word of God. On the other hand, the pietists who saw what Karl Barth really meant could also see people, whom once they had condemned as unsound, dying for their faith in the Word of God. Many a liberal scholar and a pietist were reconciled in the concentration camp of Buchenwald. Out of this experience there came a method of Bible study which owes much to both streams in the history of German church life.

NAZI PROPAGANDA

German pastors found themselves confused by the claims of the Nazi movement. It was not so much that they were unfaithful as that their vision became clouded by the successful propaganda of the State. A careful controlling of all the means of communication, a skilful use of psychology, a steady pressure in school and in social work, an offering of advantages here and disadvantages there, all the many ways in which a totalitarian state seeks to regiment the mind of its people were used especially against the German pastors. We have not yet realized how great are the powers of a totalitarian state in this battle for the mind. It cannot be easily resisted. Of course it was in Hitler's interest to get the German pastors thoroughly confused: he could not afford to have a clear-sighted leadership from the pulpit. Some pastors saw the danger more clearly than others did. They saw that their only hope was to find a standing ground outside the world in which they lived. They were not seeking a way of escape, they were seeking a standing ground from which they could face their world clearly. Contemporary theology and centuries of experience directed them to the Bible. If this had been simply a cry to read the Bible every day or an over-simplification of the problem by saying that the Bible had all the answers, it would not have given them what they needed. Hitler could deal with the Bible treated either as a book or a talisman—indeed he tried. He sponsored a positive theology which attempted to take suffering out of the list of Christian virtues; his brigade of theologians tried to use the Bible itself to further the Nazi doctrines. They even quoted the story of Christ's Passion as a reason for hating the Jews. These German pastors were wise enough to see that any printed book could be misinterpreted. They could have been as confused by Nazi propaganda about the Bible as they could be by a similar power in political matters. They therefore developed a method of Bible study which has remained Germany's greatest contribution to the biblical revival.

A NEW METHOD OF BIBLE STUDY

Groups of pastors would meet together every week to prepare their sermons. They realized that the ideas which a pastor may get in preparing his sermons alone in his study could be influenced by the pressures around him. That is a good thing in normal times, but in the Nazi period those pressures were becoming more and more pagan every day. Somehow the personal element had to be removed in preparing the sermons. The first danger was the choice of passage on which to preach. The Nazis were ready to prepare a lectionary and see to it that only those passages that supported their doctrines were used in the churches. The

Nazi church leader, Reichsbischof Möller, himself prepared a Bible with the offending passages omitted. The Church rejected that Bible before it was printed. Instead, those pastors who were seeking a new method of Bible study went back to the ancient lectionaries. They stood by the discipline of the Lutheran Church and preached on the passage chosen centuries before and whose choice therefore was in no way influenced by Nazism. They compelled themselves to take the selected passages and make them speak to their day and generation. But how? First they deputed one of their number to read all the commentaries, especially the old ones. At the meeting of pastors he would summarize what the commentaries had said. For several hours the pastors would debate the alternative interpretations. They had a thorough academic discussion such as would give joy to the heart of any liberal. Their simple question was 'What did the writer mean when he wrote this passage?' They would not move a step further until they had decided upon that. They didn't always agree, but they always knew why they had disagreed and understood the alternative interpretations. When they had thoroughly explored the background of the passage and understood its meaning, they put the Bible to one side and discussed the world in which they lived. That discussion would include the latest Nazi decrees, the impact of these upon their own people, perhaps the removal of a teacher from their school, the appointment of a new teacher, the disappearance of a neighbour. This period of discussion was earnest and real. They used their minds and their native moral sense to decide what was right and what was wrong, expecting to be better able to do this because they had just come from a detailed study of the Word of God. They tried to protect each other from making hasty comparisons, and with good German thoroughness they kept the two worlds apart as long as they could. When they had done these two jobs thoroughly they set to work to bring them together. The bringing of them together was the birth of the sermon. Of course, they did not all agree to preach the same sermon, but they had all gone through the same process, and on the whole they agreed about the way in which the particular passage studied spoke to the situation of that week. This method of Bible study combined the scrupulous work of the liberal scholar with the intense piety of the *Gemeinschaft* movement. The liberal discovered that the Bible did speak to a contemporary situation, the pietist discovered that he had to go out into the world and live there what the Bible was saying to him.

POST-WAR GERMANY

When the war was over the fruits of this method of Bible study soon became evident. These pastors had discovered in their own experience that the Word of God can be heard in the Bible really speaking to our situation. They had discovered the Bible to be the Word of God in their day. That discovery coming out of experience was far more powerful than the conclusion of a theological discussion. They discovered that the Bible was a weapon with which they could fight Nazism, and they used it in this way. But when Nazism lay in ruins it was not the kind of weapon to throw away—it was too valuable for that. Germany in her defeat brought this rich treasure into Europe. She helped men to see that the Bible speaks today. In post-war Germany this was best illustrated, not among the pastors, but among the laity who had profited from the pastors' leadership. Many a layman was troubled about the moral issues involved in an occupied Germany. None were more troubled, and to a certain extent none were more guilty, than the farmers of Germany. They had the food in their barns, while the large cities were dying of starvation, and the occupying powers naturally attempted an equitable distribution of food. Farmers found the black market a much more profitable channel for their produce than the official markets of the occupying powers—the black markets, of course, were illegal, but almost everybody used them. Christian farmers were worried not so much about the legality as about moral issues. They met in small groups to study their Bible and to discover what they should do. This was an astonishing example of confidence in the Bible to speak to our present situation. Again, under the guidance of Hanns Lilje, journalists were called together to discuss the ethics of reporting, and these discussions were carried out with a basis of Bible study. From such groups a new movement emerged in Germany which has become known as the Evangelical Academies, and today almost every province in Germany has an Academy. These are centres where laymen go to discuss the ethics of their daily life. Sometimes the discussions become very rarefied and academic, but they are always grounded in some kind of Bible study.

THE KIRCHENTAG

In a more spectacular way even than the Academies, there has come from this new method of Bible study the mass gathering of people known as the *Kirchentag*. This is a lay movement which has brought together each year or two a large number of people from different parts of

Germany. They are called not to make a political demonstration, as they had done in the days of Hitler, but to study the Bible together and to hear what God says through it to their condition. There have been great moments in the history of the Church in Germany since the war, when passages studied with all the thoroughness developed during the Nazi period have become alive for millions of Germans. The wandering of the children of Israel in the Sinai desert became a picture of the wandering refugees after the war; the prodigal son returning home, having lost everything and half afraid that he'd lost his humanity, became a picture of their own returned prisoners from Russia. There have been many such vivid parallels. They are not somebody's bright idea but the result of intense Bible study. In preparation for the *Kirchentag* a booklet is sent to all the churches who are taking part in it so that the local congregations may do their preparation week by week. They may send only one or two delegates from each parish church, but behind those delegates will be the thinking and the study of a much larger number at home. Yet even before that booklet is written the men who are going to lead the Bible study must sit down and prepare together until they have discovered what the selected passages are really saying to Germany at that time. These men are not coming to the Bible with preconceived ideas, hoping to find some passage which will support their theory. They spend two or three days together, reading the Bible, taking the specific passages which have been chosen, studying their background and, under the leadership of selected scholars, studying the context and then discussing how the passages really speak to the many people who will come together. After that preparation the churches are given the preparatory booklets in which the passages are interpreted according to different aspects of life. Thus the youth groups look specifically at youth problems. Other groups are asked to look carefully at what the passages say about family life or about industry. In each of these realms the preparatory material gives the result of group thinking and group preparation. Thus the whole German church is set in motion as it looks forward to the *Kirchentag*. When the day comes the town which is to be host is flooded with people from every part of Germany, including especially Eastern Germany. They listen to the speakers, not because they are great names, although they usually are well known, but because they have prepared themselves and they expect the Bible to say something to their condition. They are rarely disappointed. Such thorough preparation is bound to bring results. It has restored in the churches a confidence in the Bible. This *Kirchentag* is usually held in the summer, and in recent years it has been decided to hold it not annually but at less frequent intervals. The churches have said that they need longer than a year to prepare for a *Kirchentag*.

BIBLE WEEKS

Another result of this biblical movement is the Bible Week which is held in most churches in Germany once a year. In some ways this is more important for the local church than is the *Kirchentag*. Only a few people from any church can make the pilgrimage to the *Kirchentag*, but everybody can come to a Bible Week. The preparation is equally intense, although it is not arranged on a national basis. Each of the various *Landeskirche*, that is the territorial church of what might be called a province of Germany, arranges its own plan for the Bible Week. The passages are selected very carefully, sometimes from different parts of the Bible, but usually taking one long section of anything up to six or seven chapters. It may even be a whole book of the Bible. The best scholars that can be found are then asked to spend a few days together to work out the meaning of the section chosen. The section may have been chosen by the Bishop, but once he has chosen it the interpretation depends upon the hard work put into it by a small group of scholars. Their job is to find out what the writer meant, to study the contemporary situation and to expose their world to the Word of God. The result is a piece of basic writing which is then used and interpreted for various groups. A specialist on youth work must write it up in such a way that it will be helpful to youth groups. Similar work must be done for groups of men, of women, of young married couples, of industrial workers, of students, etc. Behind this specialized writing lies the basic study of the small group of scholars, and that is the all-important document. It is a careful commentary on the passage as it speaks to the real situation in that part of Germany at that time. After the basic preparation has been done and the booklets have been prepared, the local pastor must decide how he will interpret this for his people. He is expected to think in terms of his parish and its problems. Groups will meet to use the specialized material, but the heart of the Bible Week is a daily meeting, every evening from Sunday to Saturday, in which the pastor expounds the passage to his people. The result of this intensive work, year by year, is that people now expect to hear something from the Bible which relates to their situation. That is why you can find crowded churches during Bible Week. Of course, this is not true everywhere, because there are good and bad pastors in Germany as there are in any other country. There are also parishes which are much too satisfied with themselves and have no desire to hear what the Word of God says to their condition. Prosperity has done more harm to the spiritual life of Western Germany than the Nazis or the defeat ever did. To see the real importance of these Bible Weeks, you need now to go into Eastern Germany. There you will find young men who have left the Church to become Communists visiting their church again to hear one or other of the talks during Bible Week. That is the week when they expect the Church to say something which will be really important for them, even if they have deserted her. This Week is an event in the life of the church, and, when it is carried through faithfully, can expose the whole parish to the Word of God.

Apart from these two big events, the *Kirchentag* and the Bible Week, there are Bible study groups of a kind going on all the time in Germany. The material prepared for youth groups is not only used during Bible Week. It is used at camps, which in a strange way the Germans call *Freizeit* (free time), where young people spend nearly all their time studying the Bible with an excitement that is due to the relevance of the study. The young people are at it nearly all day discussing the meaning of Bible passages in relation to their life. This may sound odd for young people at camp, but the way in which the Bible passage is presented to them makes them feel that it really belongs to them and really is speaking to them. Again the value of all this material lies in the careful preparation which is done before anything is written. Apart from this careful preparation, which goes right through the German biblical movement in its groups and in its literature, the really important thing is that every

person who studies the Bible has to do the ultimate thinking for himself. Only he knows the condition to which the
Bible passage has to apply. The purpose of the method is to
expose him in his situation to the Bible passage in the most
powerful way possible.

HOLLAND

Another country whose churches have learnt much from
the bitter experiences of war and Nazi occupation is Holland. Before the war the Dutch church was a pastoral
church but seemed to have lost its real sense of mission.
Apart from individual initiative, the Dutch Reformed
Church was not aware of its need to go out into the world
and bring back those who had left it. It ignored the pagans
at home. Yet the plain fact of statistics should have roused
it to some kind of action. In 1850 it included fifty-
five per cent of the population of the Netherlands. In
1950 the figure was down to thirty-one per cent. The
bitter fact of the drift from the churches troubled some,
but not until the war, with the subsequent German occupation, did the Church itself become really aware of its
mission to the world. The vision of that mission was seen
by Dr Eijkman, Secretary of the Dutch YMCA, when he
was in Buchenwald. He was imprisoned there for his Christian activities and in particular because of his protest
against the massacre of the Jews. While in Buchenwald he
asked himself the straight question of why the German
people had chosen Hitlerism. The answer which he gave to
that was that the German church had not cared enough for
all the people. He saw the ideal Church as a Christian
totalitarianism in the best sense of the term. He wanted his
own church to care for all the people and not to be con-

cerned solely with keeping itself going. Some Christians in Holland were still prepared to maintain that their strength lay in being an isolated Christian minority with no concern for the world around them. Dr Eijkman led the Dutch Reformed Church to see its responsibility for non-Christians in factories and farms, in trade unions, in schools, in radio, in the growing industries of Holland. With money that had been saved during the war years the church established at Driebergen an institution which it called *Kerk en Wereld* (Church and World). This was to be the practical answer to how the church could best meet its responsibilities in the world. The church as a whole, including the laity, had to be reawakened, but this required leaders trained to help the laymen perform their task. This in turn required a new ministry, or, rather, a new type of ministry. The new academy of *Kerk en Wereld* was to produce this. Especially it was to train men to do social work, group work, evangelism, to reach industrial workers and also a rural population. These men were not to be ministers, they were to be laymen prepared to go wherever they were needed. They are called *Werkers in Kerkelijke Arbeid* (workers in church-sponsored activities), or as they have been popularly called, 'Wikas'. Their training includes theology, philosophy, sociology, psychology, group dynamics and case work. Throughout the country these young people are now going into factories and government offices, into farms and cities, to live as Christians in the world, going wherever the need is greatest. They are well trained and all their study is based upon the Bible. It is therefore not surprising that they have established small Bible study groups wherever they have gone. These groups are sometimes a little unusual, and there are many cases where the local pastor has disapproved of such unorthodox discussion. Yet the work of the 'Wikas' goes on and is helping forward the revival of the Dutch church.

There are many other examples of revival in Holland. With radio and with magazines the churches and the Netherlands Bible Society have been urging the people to read the Bible. In the period 1954 to 1955 a campaign known as 'The Great Trek' called upon everybody in the country to join the Church on a pilgrimage through the Bible. This was launched with all the facilities of modern communication in radio, television, film and booklets. It led to the growth of many small Bible study groups, and one of the characteristics of these was that they were thoroughly mixed. Some of them are led by laymen and they have included people from all denominations and from all levels of education. What Holland has succeeded in doing is bringing the intellectuals and the ordinary industrial workers or farm workers together in the same group. They have discovered that they could learn from each other. These groups are as varied as one can possibly imagine, but they are a real factor in stimulating a sensible Bible study. There are many examples of how reading the Bible together has led groups to take action in their local community. In Utrecht, for example, when the small Baptist church was burnt down, it was one of the groups made up of people from all denominations who began to organize a collection in all the churches to rebuild the Baptist church. Anyone who knows Holland knows how revolutionary that step was. Holland is discovering the Bible anew and finding that it reawakens spiritual life and leads to positive action. A characteristic of Dutch Bible study throughout this period has been its practical emphasis.

NORWAY

Another country which has shown signs of revival since the Second World War is Norway. Its religious life and the history of its development has been similar to that of Germany, but with some national variations. For example, the pietist movement in Norway also started about a hundred and fifty years ago when a preacher called Hans Nielsen Hauge began a revival all over the country. He was a layman, and in those days laymen were not allowed to preach in the churches. He therefore had to preach in the homes of the people or in small halls which were built specially for him. The revival was so successful that Norway soon became covered with prayer houses, but these prayer houses were not separated from the Church. They remained side by side with the church building and the same people attended both. Then about fifty years later a new revival broke out, led by a Lutheran professor of dogmatics. This bound prayer houses even more closely to the parish churches and prevented the formation of a separate denomination. None the less, there was a difference between the ordinary church members and those who regularly attended the meetings at the prayer house. The latter were narrow, and although they represented some of the best people in the parish, they tended to be argumentative and sometimes resisted the pastor. This separation within the Church continued, and the theological faculty training the ministers was divided. So Norway had two kinds of minister —the pious and the liberal. The more pious faculty has for the last twenty years had the larger number of students, and this has had the effect of increasing the influence of prayer house meetings. Today there are twelve hundred

Lutheran churches in Norway and a thousand prayer houses. In many districts the prayer houses are the only places for meeting outside the normal church services. They have been the backbone of Norwegian piety and they play a leading part still in moulding the Bible study of the parish church. They have obviously in many cases caused division because they tend to divide off the pious and holy people of a congregation from the rest.

With this background a new movement influenced Norway between the two world wars. It has variously been called the Oxford Group, Buchmanites, and later Moral Rearmament. Its influence in Scandinavia was greater than in any other part of Europe, and although it has now waned, marks of its influence can still be seen. There are few church leaders in Norway who have not at one time or another been influenced by the Oxford Group. It had the effect of bringing together the people of the prayer house and the ordinary church members. It also gave Norway a taste for the small intimate group. The opposition to the German occupation also bound the church members together, and the small groups which they had already formed as part of their church life became invaluable. There is today a growing tendency to plan the whole life of a parish and all its activities to include the holy and the not so holy in the same group. All over the country small Bible study groups are being formed, and care is always taken to get them thoroughly mixed.

When a church is first asked to form such a Bible study group there is usually resistance. As in many other parts of the world, the churches are already over-organized, and people, especially those who attend the prayer houses, have no time to attend another meeting, while the church pro-

gramme is often too full to include another item. There is
such a demand for leaders that everybody assumes no new
leader can be found for so difficult a task as leading a Bible
study group. The problem of leadership has been met by a
simple method in Norway which enables a group to be
handled without a trained leader. With this method every
member of the group prepares the passage beforehand by
reading it and putting against each verse a mark according
to the effect that verse has had upon him. If he does not
understand the verse he puts a question mark, if it strikes
him he puts an exclamation mark, if it inspires him he puts
a star. This preparation with the marked verses provides a
shared experience at the group. As the passage is read verse
by verse, each member explains why he has put a question
mark or an exclamation mark or a star. This is then the
basis for discussion, which can if necessary be supplemented
by a simple commentary. One has been prepared for this
purpose by the Church. The commentary is used only as a
last resort, because the real basis for Bible study is the
shared experience. Any member who has put an exclamation mark or a star against a verse is able to help another
member who has put a question mark. It is surprising how
much can be learned from such a simple method.

Yet even more important than this method is the setting
of the Bible study. The groups all meet in homes. The first
part of the evening is taken up with coffee and social fellowship. There is an informal discussion of the problems of the
neighbourhood, made more practical by the fact that all
members of the group come from the same area. It has
become a practice in Norway to make these groups neighbourhood groups, that is, everyone lives within a few
streets. The group is held in a different home each time so

that no one member becomes the leader of the group. The period of discussion about the neighbourhood is an important part of the Bible study. Every effort is made during that period to discover what the problems of the area are and to see whether they can be met. From experience I can say that they are very practical discussions. After this period the group begins its Bible study. At first the simple and rather superficial method of the question mark, the exclamation mark and the star proved sufficient to stimulate discussion. As the groups developed, however, there was a need for a more intensive discussion and a deeper study of the passage. To this need the Norwegian Bible Society set itself when it asked Pastor Sverre Smaadahl to tour the country in a preaching and teaching mission, to establish new neighbourhood groups and to deepen the study being carried on in the existing ones. He has arranged for the preparation of study outlines that can be used by these groups and which will lead them to a discovery of new truths. The outlines are not commentaries, they are simply suggestions of how the passage should be read, which verses should be specially noted and with which other passages they might be compared. There are now several such study outlines, each of them covering a whole course of study. They are small and do not get in the way of the unaffected Bible study which has become characteristic of these groups. Today there are about two thousand groups throughout Norway, and eighty per cent of them have moved over from the simpler method of preparation to the study outlines.

SCOTLAND

In Scotland before the Second World War a movement

started on the island of Iona which has had important consequences for British church life and has contributed much
to the rediscovery of the meaning of community. Scottish
ministers had a way of appearing vastly superior to their
lay brethren. Versed in theology, they seemed like beings
apart. 'The minister' was someone high and lifted up. At
least, so his people thought, and so he himself began to
believe. Then during the period of the nineteen-thirties a
Scottish Presbyterian minister in an industrial parish saw
the stupidity of this separateness and began to get down
beside his people. He saw that ministers must come close
to the problems of daily work, and he saw also that on the
island of Iona there was an opportunity to blend manual
work with theology and worship because there stood an
ancient cathedral in ruins. George MacLeod called on his
fellow ministers and laymen to stand together and with
their own hands rebuild the Abbey on Iona. From that
desire to bring ministers into real contact with manual
work and the problems of modern society has sprung the
Iona Community. It is not a religious order as the Catholic
Church uses the term, neither is it an attempt to revive the
monastic life in Protestantism. It is simply an association
of ministers and laity who continue their daily work and
in it seek to discover together the meaning of the 'Christian
community' for today. The Community is now old enough
to have influenced the Church of Scotland considerably.
It has sent an army of young ministers into the parishes of
Scotland, particularly the industrial parishes, with a new
determination to reconcile the Scots to their Church again.
They have done much, and the effect is seen in the ordinary life of the parish. Kitchen kirks, as they are called,
abound, where neighbours meet together in friendly fashion

to discuss the problems of their neighbourhood and eventually to study their Bible together. They resemble very closely the neighbourhood groups of Norway.

It was from these men that the best support came for a Radio Mission carried through in 1950 by BBC Scotland. This was an attempt to use all the resources of radio to win the people of Scotland for Christ. It was planned with a team of broadcasters and preachers. Over the space of six weeks all the normal periods devoted to religious broadcasting were given over to the Radio Mission. Two of the presbyteries in Scotland had local missions at the same time which were carefully geared into the programmes. Publicity was used locally and for six weeks the campaign went on intensively. The story of that campaign has been written by R. H. W. Falconer in a book which he called *Success and Failure of a Radio Mission.* His title was well chosen because the Radio Mission both succeeded and failed. It succeeded in so far as it persuaded the Church of Scotland that radio could be used in this way. Almost every year since that date the Church of Scotland has co-operated fully with the BBC to put on something like the first Radio Mission. Indeed, today almost the whole of Scottish broadcasting is so closely linked with the Church of Scotland that it amounts to a continuous mission of the Church to the people. The failure was the mistaken aim. Although the Mission defined itself as having a threefold aim, to win those who were outside the Church, to reclaim the lapsed and to strengthen the faithful, most of those engaged in the Mission had as their main purpose to win people from outside. In effect very few people were won from outside because in Scotland hardly anybody is outside the Church. That does not mean that a large number of people go to church, but it does mean that almost everybody regards himself as attached in some way to one or other of the churches in Scotland, predominantly the Church of Scotland. Thus a new atmosphere was determined by the experience of this Mission. Those who do not go to church must be considered not as outside the Church but as lapsed.

Arising out of the Iona Community, the Radio Mission and other movements of the Spirit in Scotland, there came the 'Tell Scotland Movement' which has been responsible for very much in church life during the past few years. It was this movement which invited Billy Graham to Scotland and put on his platform theological professors, church leaders and representatives of some of the fundamentalist groups. The Tell Scotland Movement is an ecumenical movement but very naturally the largest part of it is Church of Scotland. It was responsible for arranging a Kirk Week on the pattern of the German *Kirchentag* in 1957 and an ecumenical conference on 'Scotland Faces the World's Need' in the same year. It held its second Kirk Week in Dundee in 1959.

These outstanding demonstrations of a new spiritual life in Scotland are reflected also at the parish level. Particularly among those ministers who have been members of the Iona Community there has developed a revival of the Elders' meetings. This is a kind of house church but based upon an old pattern. The Elders are part of the administrative structure of the Church of Scotland. Their function was to rule, rather like civil magistrates, and this function had been lost. They had to find a new function as ordained laymen. They discovered that they had left the teaching and the pastoral work to the minister, which was another part of the separateness that had afflicted the Church of

Scotland. It was not always so, because the Elder should have exercised a pastoral function, and this function is now being revived. The number of Elders has been increased in many parishes, and each is given pastoral responsibility for a certain geographical area of the parish, usually the area in which he lives. It is his function not only to see that the members in his area support the church, but also to see that their spiritual life is deepened. In his own home he will gather together the members from his area and lead them in Bible study. The main concern behind such a meeting in the home is to serve the area, and the Bible study is seen in that context. The whole idea can be missed if it is merely a pious group studying the Bible. The danger then is that the members begin to enjoy it and imagine that they are doing something specially good and holy in having long discussions about the Bible. As everywhere, they are much more ready to do this than to help their neighbour. As one minister wrote, when describing the meetings in his parish, 'Often the person who enjoys disputing about texts is not the person who carries out the work of the church. The whole house church movement must be relentlessly related to practical service, or it is in danger of becoming just another exclusive church-centred idea.'

Another minister who was trying to explain the part which the Bible plays in the house meetings in his parish said that his Elders' meetings had grown out of Bible study groups which had failed. These groups had been rather precious and did nothing but Bible study. Members who attended them with the best of intentions found them too difficult and found that they accentuated the educational differences between the members of the group. When the new form was evolved he had to promise that there would be no Bible study. So the house meetings started in his parish with no intention of becoming Bible study groups and certainly were not a carefully devised plan for trapping people into reading their Bibles. His groups anyway have been concerned with people and life. He writes about them: 'I'm increasingly chary of Bible study groups for the simple reason that the Bible has been more alive in groups concerned about people and life than in groups concerned about the Bible.' It is typical of such groups as his that although they began by promising no Bible study, they had not long been formed when all the members were seeking to know more about Christianity and therefore turning to the Bible. In the course of one year the assistant minister was asked to visit several groups to help them in a study of Amos, and the minister had to do the same thing with a number of other groups on Ephesians. These house meetings or Elders' meetings have not spread to all the parishes of Scotland by any means, but so far as statistics can be determined there are now about three hundred of them in different parts of Scotland.

THE MINISTER'S PART

For effective Bible study, lay leadership is essential although the minister must take part. With an ordinary church group led by the average minister, the people will tend to listen to him as the expert. They will enjoy hearing his explanation of the meaning of a passage and they will be pleased that he has illuminated it for them in a way that they could not do for themselves, but it is unlikely that they will have an opportunity to relate the problems of their daily life as they see them to the Word of God as it is heard in the passage. The whole study is liable to become simply an instruction. Instruction has its part in church life, but it is not depth Bible study. The minister too will tend to approach the passage on the basis of his own training and his own experiences. His training will be academic and his experiences will tend to be special, not those of his people. Therefore, while the minister's specialized knowledge is of great use in a Bible study group, his leadership may prevent that depth Bible study which is necessary for the people. Lay leadership, on the other hand, suffers from lack of instruction. It could be that a lively leader would get a group to discuss the problems which interest them all without seriously relating those problems to any understanding of the passage.

In the examples of really effective Bible study which have already been quoted in this chapter, several weaknesses can be noted. The German Bible study tended to be too much in the hands of the pastors and, although the *Kirchentag* is a lay movement with a lay leader, the Bible study is conducted by an expert—a theologian. Efforts are made to see that the pastors in Germany are well informed about the real problems of their people, but the failure to discover lay leadership for Bible study is a weakness which needs to be overcome. On the other hand, the early neighbourhood groups in Norway often failed to understand the passage they were studying. Even the shared experience was often a sharing of ignorance. It is for that reason that the study outlines are being so quickly accepted. Even in Scotland it has been very difficult to discover lay initiative in Bible study. One of the things which came out of the Radio Mission was the discovery that unless the minister

B

took the lead nothing happened. What then is required in effective Bible study is lay leadership instructed by the minister.

In Scotland this has been attempted through the Elders' meetings. Where these are working properly as Bible study groups, the minister has a regular meeting with the Elders to discuss how the Bible passages are being applied. This is a valuable opportunity for him to give the Elders the necessary equipment for serious Bible study. Lay leadership always needs this kind of stiffening. There are books and pamphlets which will help to do this, but they are most valuable when they are supplemented by help from the local minister. Giving this help also brings the minister closer to the Bible study groups and helps him to do his own pastoral work more effectively. It is good too if he can visit some of the groups, not as a leader but as an observer to whom the people can turn if they are in real difficulty about the exegesis of a verse.

THE DANGER OF SEPARATION

Bible study is really effective only when it is related to the background conditions of the people in the group. This is not secured by a lay leader, because laymen as well as ministers can take Bible study into an atmosphere quite unrelated to their daily life. The weakness of the Bible study among pietists was that they were separated from the world and did not relate what they found in the Bible to what happened in their world around them. All the effective Bible study groups that have been mentioned in this chapter include an attempt, more or less successful, to thrust the world into the group. The Norwegian neighbourhood groups with their initial coffee period is one way to do it; the German method of putting the Bible to one side and discussing the problems of the neighbourhood in the middle part of their study is another and more thorough way of doing it. Some groups will rely upon literature to force the members to ask relevant questions of the passage. This has been done particularly well by certain conservative groups in Holland. Also certain intellectual groups in Germany, of students and ex-students, have their own publication helping them always to relate the passage they are studying to problems of the cultural world in which they live. However it is done, there is no effective Bible study which does not take seriously the background conditions of the people in the group.

LEARNING FROM ONE ANOTHER

Every country has its own history, and it will be clear from the examples already given that the different countries have also developed different methods as the result of their histories. An examination of these methods shows that there is a great deal of rich experience available for anyone who wants to begin Bible study, but the question remains whether methods can be transferred from one country to another. Certainly precautions must be taken before any successful experiment is hailed as an ideal method for all the world. When I first realized the value of the *Kirchentag* in Germany and recommended to the English churches that they should undertake a similar enterprise, it was immediately pointed out to me that the *Kirchentag* was very German and could not be taken across the English Channel. There was much wisdom in this, because English church life is totally different from German church life. For one thing, the various denominations in England could not work together so easily as in Germany. The *Kirchentag* requires one denomination which is at least dominant, and the scattered resources of the churches in England made this difficult.

A parallel was however found in Scotland, where despite the presence of the Episcopal Church of Scotland and other Free Churches, the Church of Scotland is the dominant denomination in a way that the Church of England is not in England. In 1957 Scotland held its first Kirk Week in Aberdeen, and in preparation for this a study was made of the German *Kirchentag*. The Scottish Kirk Week was different, but it had the essential idea of the German *Kirchentag*. There was intensive preparation and the basis of the Week was Bible study. The main obvious difference was that Scotland decided upon Bible study in smaller groups, and therefore they required a larger number of leaders for Bible study. It was a successful experiment, and much was learnt that would enable Scotland to carry through a second Kirk Week with even greater success. This was held in July 1959, and this time some definite alterations were made as a result of the experience of the first. This time there was only the minimum of public exposition of the Scriptures to mass audiences. Instead the time was taken up with real Bible study groups under lay leaders working on passages related to the theme of the day. It had been decided that the main theme should be on the lines of 'The People of God' facing 'The Crisis of Man'. The very nature of Kirk Week requires that there should be some public speaking, and for this the best men that could be found were brought to Kirk Week to speak on their own subject. This provided material for the discussions which went on in the smaller groups. Laity workshops also helped delegates to discover the full meaning of a Christian vocation. But the whole structure of the Week was based on Bible study. Nearly a thousand laymen came to the Kirk Week to study the Bible for themselves. They were led by laymen in their own small groups, although some of the speakers at the public meetings were ministers. Before Kirk Week began these lay leaders were prepared by intensive Bible study and in fact went through a process similar to that of the pastors in Nazi Germany, who studied their Bibles together to find out how they could combat Nazism. They demonstrated that a crisis was not necessary to produce effective Bible study. Or perhaps it was that they discerned that a Christian in this world is always living in a crisis. The experience of Kirk Week sent leaders and others back to their churches to continue Bible study on the same passages, and notes have since been prepared to enable all to lead groups.

In a much quieter way a small West of England town prepared itself to learn from the experiences of the German Bible Week. This experiment was carried through in Yeovil, Somerset, in December 1958. First there was consultation with all the ministers in the town. It was important for an English town that this should be ecumenial and not the work of one denomination. For this reason the co-operation of all the ministers was sought and it was gladly given. Anglican and Free Church ministers were informed about the methods of German Bible study, and after careful discussion they decided that they would support the experiment of a similar Bible Week in Yeovil with all their resources. When they had clearly understood what this involved, the first step was to select the passage for study. The date for the Bible Week had been set between the Second and Third Sundays in Advent and it seemed therefore natural to choose an Advent theme. The Book of the Revelation seemed a good choice, but on further discussion it was decided that this would rouse too many peripheral discussions. Instead, four parables of the Kingdom were chosen. When selected they were given to two younger ministers, one Anglican, one Free Church, to prepare the basic commentary material. They had to read all the commentaries and present papers indicating the various interpretations that had been given of the parables. In September the ministers met for a day of study and preparation, more or less on the German pattern. The first part of the day was spent in academic study, securing good exegesis of the four parables, the second part on a discussion of the problems facing the people of Yeovil, the third part bringing the two worlds together—the world of daily life and the world of these four parables. This was an attempt to expose the problems of Yeovil to the Word of God as we hear it in four parables of the Kingdom. That provided the basic preparation for the Bible Week. Apart from the usual publicity, there was preparation of the people in all the churches, disturbing their normal pattern of activity as little as possible. The ministers prepared themselves to preach on the Second Sunday in Advent. On that day these four parables constituted the basis of sermons preached from every pulpit in the town. On the four successive evenings each of the parables was expounded to a combined congregation in the largest church of the town. There was discussion for those who wanted it, but the main thing was to present these parables in such a way that they really spoke to the condition of the people in Yeovil. The support for this Bible Week was greater than anyone had expected. The discussion hall was crowded every night, as laymen spoke and tried to discover what God was saying to them in Yeovil. The churches discovered a new unity, the people realized their common responsibility, and God spoke. This was an English Bible Week, but it had learnt much from the German experience along the same lines.

THE BASIC PRINCIPLES

From these two examples it is clear that an experiment in one country which has proved successful can be transferred, with the necessary modifications, to another country and culture. They showed also that a political crisis, which had given an opportunity for the initial discovery, was not essential if men were to learn from it in another country. It is not true that the Bible only comes alive in critical times, unless we assume that all times are critical. There are many more less ambitious examples. Many a man has caught an idea during his travel in a foreign country and gone back to his home church and introduced that idea in the setting of his home. Much more could be done in learning from one another. For example, the peoples of Europe could learn a great deal from the adult Sunday School movements in the USA, as well as from the Vacation Bible Schools. The whole organization of these could not be lifted and put down in any European country, but with suitable modifications their essential principles could be learnt and could benefit the churches of Europe. The experiences of the churches of the world belong to the whole Church of Christ and should be appropriated. This does not always mean the copying of an experiment. It may mean the studying of experiments and discovering from them what are the basic principles of effective Bible study. These basic principles will be all the more valuable if they can be reduced in number. I shall therefore attempt to deduce from the experiments which I have studied three basic principles.

1. Bible study should be at considerable depth. There is no place in effective Bible study for a superficial examination of the text. All the work which the liberal theologians did, in examining the text, writing critical commentaries and exploring the background information, needs to be taken into consideration in our study of the Bible. The liberal movements in theology may have had a bad time recently, but it would be foolish to ignore the positive results of their Bible study. We need therefore to use the best commentaries, and academic study still has its place within our study of the Bible. No man can begin to discover what the Bible is saying to his situation until first of all he knows what it means and what it was saying to the situation for which it was written. This depth Bible study will require the asking of a number of essential questions.

First, what happened? An effective Bible study needs to be quite honest and, if necessary, needs to discover that the passage is inaccurate. It may be that the account of an event in the Bible is thoroughly biased. It is important to know the reason for the bias and to be able to compare the biblical account with the best that historical research can give to us of what really happened. The Bible must not be above criticism. Properly used, that criticism can bring us to a deeper understanding of the Bible. The second question is, 'What does it mean?' A full knowledge of the background to a Bible statement may be essential if we are to grasp the real meaning of a verse. It may be much easier to jump at a superficial meaning, but to do so will mean missing what that passage is saying to us. This also will require honesty. A man who has used a verse either in preaching or in argument, and then discovers that the verse could not possibly have meant what he had made it mean, must be prepared to accept the new insight. This requires hard work and honesty. The third question is, 'Why did the writer give us this passage?' Almost every writer in the Bible had a large amount of material from which to select. In making his selection the writer always had some reason. If we can discern that reason we are beginning to get to the heart of the passage. Effective Bible study is always depth Bible study.

2. Bible study must be related to the situation in which the people find themselves. All traditions have neglected this principle. The pietists have separated themselves from the world and the liberals have sometimes been guilty of enjoying the Bible apart from its real applications. We have all fallen short, but an analysis of really effective Bible study shows that in every case there was an attempt made to relate the insights of the Bible study group to the world outside. This can only be done by a constant asking of questions. When we have discovered what the passage means, we need to go further and say, 'What does it mean to me?' Now the danger of such a question is that it will still remain within the purely personal realm. The Church has long experience of dealing with personal problems and a rather bad experience of dealing with public problems. There are groups in some parts of Europe where the members after studying the passage go out and try to live by that passage during the coming week. They then report

back on how they have fared. This may not be the best way to do it, but at least it thrusts into the group every week the kind of questions which you must ask if you are going to live by the passage you are studying in the real world. So that the question becomes more than, 'What does this passage say to me?' It becomes, 'What will this passage say to me tomorrow when I am at my work?'

3. Bible study is at its best when it is group thinking. Of course the centuries have many examples of the way in which a man alone can hear the Word of God through the Bible. The stories of prisons and concentration camps tell us constantly of how powerful Bible study can be under such conditions. Yet in general it remains true that the best Bible study is done when a group of people are met together, determined to find out what the Bible means to them. There are many obvious reasons for this principle. Individually you are more inclined to look in the Bible for things that will support your own idea. A group can correct this, because different members will have different ideas. A man alone with his Bible, even when he is supplied with the best commentaries, is only getting instruction from others, whereas in a group he is getting encounter with them. All the examples of Bible study which have been really effective suggest that the disciplined use of group thinking will make the Word of God sound more clearly from the passage than any book or individual thinker can. The experience of the Germans under the Nazis seems to me to be decisive on this point.

2

HOW TO BEGIN A BIBLE STUDY GROUP

THE older cookery books began their recipes with such instructions as 'First catch your hare'. Just as you cannot have a jugged hare without a hare, you cannot have group Bible study without a group. Of course a group is not the only form of Bible study, but it is the most effective way to dig deeply into the meaning of the Bible for people in this generation. Personal Bible study will still continue, but it will tend to be the receiving of instruction from those who have written books about the Bible. Those who use the many booklets prepared by such organizations as the International Bible Reading Association, the Scripture Union and the Bible Reading Fellowship will acquire a great deal of information. They will know the answers which scholars give to some of the more important questions raised about the Bible. If they continue or follow a course laid down by Bishop Stephen Neill for the BRF, they will end up with a well-informed mind. All this is important. There is a value in personal Bible study which can go beyond this. Many of the Bible reading helps mentioned above have been written to help people answer the basic question, What does this passage say to me in my life? All this is Bible study, but there is a need to go further which only a group can meet. Therefore effective Bible study requires a group. This may be difficult but it is not impossible

—there are very few churches which could not, if they tried, bring together a group of people for Bible study.

REASONS FOR MEETING

The first thing to remember in bringing together the group is that they need not be brought together specifically for Bible study. Perhaps it is better that they should not. Those who come together, eager to study the Bible, are often people of a certain type and not a good cross-section of an average congregation. Bible study is at its best when it is not planned but grows out of the needs of a group already meeting. So to catch your group means to find out first of all if there is a reason why people want to meet together. The reasons may be as varied as the districts in which people live. There may be a local concern about the conditions of living, there may be simply a need for friendship among lonely people. During the war in Britain people often met together because of the air-raids. Despite Government instructions not to meet together in groups but to disperse as much as possible, the natural instinct to get together in time of danger formed groups all over the country, and some of these became Bible study groups. In a new area where houses have been erected for the first time and people have come together from different towns and villages, there is often no centre of community. There is a need for people to meet together to create a social stability. Mothers may often come together because they have common concerns about their children, or even about their husbands. In one street in Amsterdam, newly-built and with all the neighbours complete strangers, several people found themselves coming on to the street at about the same time every Sunday morning. They were all going to different churches, but they had this one thing in common, that they emerged at roughly the same time and met each other in the street. That seems a very slender reason for coming together, but it brought them together into a group which was at first casual and later became a good Bible study group. It hardly matters why a group comes together. There are very few causes which can hold a group together indefinitely, and human nature is such that if the people like each other they will want to find a reason for meeting. These groups are natural groupings and far better for Bible study than a specially selected group of people who are intensely interested in the Bible.

TIME AND PLACE

The time and place of meeting will have to be determined according to local conditions, and may well have been settled before a group becomes a Bible study group. The important thing is to make it as natural a place of meeting as possible and to fix the time according to the needs of the group. There is nothing sacred about place or time for Bible study. If it is a group of mothers who have been meeting in the morning over coffee to discuss the problems of their children, they should be encouraged to continue to meet at the same time and the same place, which is presumably in their homes. The reason for this is to preserve the continuity as far as possible. It would be a loss if they stopped talking about their children as soon as they started studying the Bible. Most Bible study groups will be in the evenings when the day's work is done, or on Sundays. Usually it is best to meet in different homes, but there is

45

a certain advantage in meeting on church premises. A Bible study group has to look both ways: towards the Church and towards the world. So long as a strong contact can be maintained with the church then the group should meet in members' homes, but if there is a danger that the group is separating from the ordinary life of the church it may be as well to move it to a small room on church premises. If the church develops a number of Bible study groups, it will then become necessary to meet in homes, and usually it is as well to avoid meeting every time in the same home. There are of course exceptions to this, and local conditions must be the final deciding factor. The actual Bible study should usually last about an hour, but it can be much more effective if the whole evening is given over to the meeting of the group. There will be more to say about the division of time during the meeting later in this chapter.

LEADERSHIP

Almost the first question that arises with a Bible study group is the question of leadership. It is usually assumed that the leader has to know a great deal more about the Bible than the other members of the group do, hence the next logical step is to ask the minister to lead it. That is nearly always fatal, although there are exceptions. A moment's reflection will assure anyone that a church which hopes to have a number of Bible study groups will need to develop a lay leadership sooner or later. It is as well to begin that way and have lay leadership even for the first Bible study group that grows up in a church. Although it is not true that the leader needs to know a great deal more about the Bible than the other members do, it is true that the leader needs some kind of training. It is in the training that the minister's part can be played with greatest value. He should always be available to discuss with the leader or leaders of his Bible study groups the problems which arise in those groups. He may sometimes feel that it would be simpler if he led the group himself, but there is something which a layman can do in Bible study which cannot be done by the minister. When the lay leader and the minister discuss the problems that have been raised by a Bible study group they discuss on a basis of equality, not of teacher and taught. Both have something to bring to discussion which helps them to arrive at conclusions together. The minister has his specialized training, which he makes available to the lay leader. The lay leader has his close association with the world and his nearness to the members of the group. The group will deal with him as one of themselves; they will be less inclined to sit back and wait to have information poured into them. This discussion between minister and lay leader should be at regular intervals and not just sporadic. Even when there is only one Bible study group in a church it is necessary for the leader to have this constant consultation, both for the sake of the group whose problems can be helped by the minister, and for the sake of the minister who can in this way keep his link with the thinking of the group. Naturally arrangements will differ from district to district, but some mechanism of this kind needs to be worked out to secure two things : lay leaders must be trained, and the link between the Bible study groups and the on-going life of the church must be strongly established.

The qualities required in a leader are that he should be honest, be able to read and think and, most important of all, be able to keep quiet while others are talking. It is not the function of the leader to instruct but to help guide discussion. He will supply the group with all the necessary information as it is required; he will report upon his talks with the minister if they have concerned some special problem of the group; he will sometimes open up the discussion on a Bible passage. Some leaders prefer to do this every time, but it is generally to be preferred that they depute to various members of the group the task of opening up the discussion. When a church can provide it, there should be a training course for leaders of Bible study groups with the same kind of thoroughness as there is for the training of Sunday school teachers. This may not be possible, and the regular meeting with the minister will have to suffice. The lay leader needs to be kept fully informed about necessary literature. A great deal is published by the various publishing houses and he could easily become lost amidst the mass of material available. The minister can also help him by suggesting which books are likely to be important for his work. He should not be submerged in books lest he make himself into an academic expert and lose one of his greatest qualities in being one of the group. He should on the whole be better informed than the rest of the group, but not so far ahead that he has lost contact with their problems. Again it needs to be remembered that his function is not that of instructor. He joins with them in a search for the meaning of the Bible passage. He is likely to learn as much if not more than any member of the group.

RETAINING INTEREST

As with any other activity, Bible study will only keep a group so long as it is getting somewhere. The Bible study which begins as a novel experience and keeps the members interested without digging deep into the meaning of the passage will soon lose the interest of the better members of the group. For this reason, and because Bible study is a serious occupation, it is necessary to secure depth as soon as possible. It will be easier to assure depth Bible study if it is started from the beginning than it will be to introduce it into a superficial Bible study group which has been going on a long time. The group can usually be persuaded that if Bible study is worth doing it is worth working at. To meet and try to guess the meaning of a passage may be an interesting parlour game but is not Bible study. Even when the method used in Norway of sharing experiences by putting question mark, exclamation mark, star, against different verses yielded some fruitful discussion, it soon had to be abandoned because it was not digging deep enough into the meaning of the passage. A sharing of impressions about a Bible passage is not enough. The members wish to discover new truths and to become better informed about their Bible. If the study remains at a superficial level, the more intelligent members will tend to pursue their own personal Bible study and drift away from the group. This will be a loss both to the group and to themselves. A superficial Bible study also allows too much opportunity to people who speak easily and tend to monopolize the evening. Leader and group must be persuaded that they are undertaking a difficult task which will be rewarding if they work at it. It must also be made clear that working at it is possible for all members of the group. The educational differences which sometimes appear in groups must not be allowed to divide the group. The man who has read widely needs in some way to be brought on to the level of the person who has hardly ever read a whole book in his life. This can be done if both are conducted to the same material which is for both of them new material, and if both can be limited to discussing that material common to them both. The 'Great Books Foundation' in the USA realized the wisdom of this when they required that their discussion groups should discuss only the material which had been provided for the reading of all. Bible study groups can learn from that experience, but should not go quite so far. It is important that no member should feel that his educational standard is too low for him to join in the Bible study group. Yet discussion is only possible if the members are allowed to draw upon both their experience and their reading. A wise leader will see to it that they do not draw too much upon reading that is unknown to the group. He will do this more easily if the new material to which all have been introduced is sufficiently absorbing.

The choice of that material is very important indeed but it cannot be done for every group in the country. Here the minister and the leader should take careful consultation. The material must be such as all will be able to understand provided they work at it. It should not be popular material which has attempted to simplify too much. It is far better if the group is directed to a solid commentary and has to work through it. The Layman's Bible Commentary is an obvious choice, and it would be good for a group to possess the volume containing the passages they are studying. In some churches, however, the minister may feel able to give time to summarizing one of the more detailed commentaries which he could not ask a Bible study group to work through. Whether the group uses the Layman's Commentary, or a summary made by the minister of some technical commentary, what it is looking for is the exegesis. The material provided, whether in the form of a volume or a summary, will be the possession of the group for a long time. They may spend as much as three months on one book of the Bible. During that time it will not be expected or even desired that every member of the group should read the commentary. One member will be deputed each time to prepare the lesson. It will not always be the same member. A wise leader will see to it that every one of the group has his opportunity to present to the whole group what the commentary says about the passage. This helps to secure some depth in the study, but one danger must be carefully avoided. The group has not met to discover what the commentary means, it has met to discover what the Bible says. The commentary has simply given some material which will enable the group to discuss along firm and fairly authentic lines. At least it will prevent them from going hopelessly astray.

Even more important than the commentary is that they themselves should be open to the Word of God when they have understood what it means. It is the function of the commentary and that extra information which the minister may have given to the leader that helps to carry through the first of the three basic principles outlined at the end of the last chapter: 'Bible study should be at considerable depth.' But the phrase 'depth Bible study' refers to something more than the exegesis of the passage. It must include that because there is no depth Bible study based upon a false or superficial exegesis. The whole group must be prepared to relate whatever they discover the passage really means to their situation. This becomes a cumulative process. It requires a good deal of hard work to give your mind to the proper exegesis of a passage, but that hard work is seen to be worth while when the passage is related to daily living. A group will work if it knows that what it discovers will help daily life. You can sustain an interest in academic discussion for a time through curiosity, but continuous Bible study will only go on if it is related to life.

PARTICIPATION

This leads to one of the early problems facing any Bible study group. Interest must be maintained and there must be participation from all members of the group. The two things are linked. There will be participation if there is real interest and real interest is only sustained if there is participation. The leader and the minister will often be discussing this very problem. New methods must constantly be introduced and the slightest sign of a flagging of interest must be noted, analysed and checked. A Bible study may have many faults and may go on having these faults, but it can never afford to be dull. Among the many methods that will be used to encourage participation and sustain interest is the method of using different translations of the Bible. Most groups should do their basic study from the Revised Standard Version, but it would be a good thing if there were several other versions among members of the group. If a group is not too large it should be possible for every member to have a different translation. Today there should be enough translations to go round a group of nearly twenty, at least so far as the New Testament is concerned, and no group should be bigger than that. The value of these various translations is that they stimulate members to make comments. For example, if a group were studying the Acts 8, the leader would presumably be using the Revised Standard

Version. Let us imagine that different members of the group had the Authorized Version, the Riverside New Testament, the New Testament in Plain English by Charles Kingsley Williams, *The Young Church in Action* by J. B. Phillips, The Twentieth Century New Testament, Weymouth and the translation of the Acts by C. H. Rieu. The leader would come eventually to the point where Peter rebukes Simon because he wishes to purchase the gift of the Spirit, or rather the power to give the Spirit, with money. The leader reads:

But Peter said to him, 'Your silver perish with you, because you thought you could obtain the gift of God with money! You have neither part nor lot in this matter, for your heart is not right before God. Repent therefore of this wickedness of yours, and pray to the Lord that, if possible, the intent of your heart may be forgiven you. For I see that you are in the gall of bitterness and in the bond of iniquity.' (RSV)

Various members of the group will have in front of them that passage translated in this way:

But Peter said unto him, Thy money perish with thee, because thou hast thought that the gift of God may be purchased with money. Thou hast neither part nor lot in this matter: for thy heart is not right in the sight of God. Repent therefore of this thy wickedness, and pray God, if perhaps the thought of thine heart may be forgiven thee. For I perceive that thou art in the gall of bitterness, and in the bond of iniquity. (Authorized Version)

or:

But Peter said to him, 'Your money perish with you because you have thought that you could buy the gift of God with money! You have no part or lot in this matter. For your heart is not right before God. Repent of this wickedness of yours, and pray the Lord that, if possible, the though of your heart may be forgiven you. For I see that

you are in the gall of bitterness and the fetters of unrighteousness.' (Riverside New Testament)

or :

But Peter said to him, 'A curse on you and your money,
because you thought you could buy the free gift of God.
There is no part nor portion for you in this word; for your
heart is not right before God. Repent, therefore, of this
wickedness and pray to the Lord, that the intention of your
heart may be forgiven; for I see that you are bitter as gall
and chained by sin.' (The New Testament in Plain English)

or :

But Peter said to him, 'To hell with you and your money!
How dare you think you could buy the gift of God? You
can have no share or place in this ministry, for your heart
is not honest before God. All you can do now is to repent
of this wickedness of yours and pray earnestly to God that
the evil intention of your heart may be forgiven. For I can
see inside you, and I see a man bitter with jealousy and
bound with his own sin!' (*The Young Church in Action*)

or :

'Take your money to perdition with you!' Peter exclaimed,
'for thinking God's free gift could be bought with gold! You
have no share or part in our Message for your heart is not
right with God. So repent of this wickedness of yours, and
pray to the Lord, that, if possible, you may be forgiven for
such a thought; for I see that you have fallen into bitter
jealousy and are in bondage to iniquity.' (Twentieth Century New Testament)

or :

'Perish your money and yourself,' replied Peter, 'because
you have imagined that you can obtain God's free gift with
money! No part or lot have you in this matter, for your
heart is not right in God's sight. Repent, therefore, of this
wickedness of yours, and pray to the Lord, in the hope that
the purpose which is in your heart may perhaps be forgiven

you. For I perceive that you have fallen into the bitterest bondage of unrighteousness.' (Weymouth)
or :

'Perdition take you and your money,' said Peter, 'for thinking that you could buy the gift of God! These matters are beyond your grasp. You cannot see things in their true light. Repent of your sin, and say your prayers to the Lord in the hope that you may be forgiven for your wicked scheme. It shows how sunk and degraded you are.' (Rieu)

It is easy to see how the slight variants in the text would cause immediate comment. This comment would lead to a comparing of the different translations and raise the question why certain translators had done it one way and why others had used quite different phrases. Such a discussion will invariably lead to a better understanding of the original text, and that is always good in Bible study. While the use of various versions creates a continuing stimulus to discussion, there must be other means employed also to keep the interest. Some leaders will choose only a selected number of passages in a short series for study. Others will see to it that only short books of the Bible are studied in the early period. Any sense of weariness must be excluded. The steady ploughing through the Bible from cover to cover is quite impossible in such a study group.

RELEVANCE

It is equally important that members of the group should realize that their own questions are being answered in their Bible study. It is not enough to raise new questions and answer them. People come to a Bible study group with their own problems, and it is not the purpose of the group to keep them preoccupied so that they will not concern themselves with their own problems. A leader will be sensitive to the needs of the group and if he finds that the pace of Bible study is going too quickly he will pause for the consideration of specific problems. It may, for example, be necessary to take two or three sessions on some question which has been raised by the passage under study. To go on with the next passage when certain questions have not been answered is to create a feeling of frustration. Members get the impression that they are being hurried through a book of the Bible which must be finished according to schedule. Although it is good that they should finish the book they are studying, it is far more important that the problems raised should be seriously dealt with. A study of one of the Synoptic Gospels, for example, would probably have to pause for several sessions when it came to the Temptations in order to discuss thoroughly what part the devil plays in our thinking today.

OPENNESS

One of the most frustrating things about Bible study groups is caused by the feeling that all the answers are known somewhere. The problem then becomes reduced to a game of discovering who knows them or where they are written up. Serious Bible study cannot continue long on this assumption. It must be clear to the group that they are making new discoveries, that there are things about the Bible which have not been known before. Naturally they will need help from people who have studied the passage before them, but they can take that study further. Studying the Bible is like an exploration. It builds upon the work of earlier explorers, but its real purpose is to discover new territory or to map out in greater detail territory which has been discovered. The leader can do a great deal to create this atmosphere of exploration. He must refrain from any action which sounds like giving the correct answer after the discussion has gone on long enough. There is nothing worse than the patronizing leader who allows a discussion to go on for the good of the members but makes clear that he knew the correct answer all the time. Leader and group together must venture into the unknown if this is to be real Bible study.

THE REAL WORLD

Another important factor in the development of effective Bible study is that it should be rooted in the real world in which members live. Every possible method must be used to prevent discussion from becoming separated from the everyday life of the member. This can be done by establishing at the very beginning a method of sharing experiences. Although the superficial method of Bible study, which required simply the putting of question mark, exclamation mark and star, did not dig deep enough into the meaning of the passage, it provided one thing that every Bible study group needs. It gave the members an opportunity of saying how the verse had impressed them when they were preparing it in their own homes. Of course, even this could be separated from the world in which they lived, but it stood less chance of being separated if it was prepared when they were away from the fellowship of likeminded people. So the means that is used to prepare the passage may also help the member to keep his mind on the world in which he lives. The leader should encourage every member to think of the verse or even the chapter which he is reading in relation to his work, his home, his family and his relations with other people. The group can go even further than this because they can discuss the relation of the passage to the community life and even to the political life of their country.

CONFIDENCE

Every Bible study group sooner or later runs into the difficulty of avoiding extremes in cases like this. Experiences must be shared, but this does not mean providing a platform for everybody to talk about himself. The political life of a country should often be discussed, but this does not mean that the group should turn into a discussion group on matters of political interest with occasional references to the Bible. There is a difficult course between extremes to be steered here. It will have to be steered by the leader, although he does well to take the group into his confidence so that they know where they are being steered. He needs to show that the basic reason for study is that he believes and wants them to believe too that the Bible has something to say to contemporary life. Somehow this confidence in the relevance of the Bible has to be established, or all the methods used to relate it to everyday life will fail. If, fundamentally, the group do not really believe that the Bible has anything to say in an industrial community, then they will never come round to good Bible study. The group may of course have doubts and almost certainly will—members may wonder how on earth the Book of Judges can say anything in a Welfare State—but if in some way a confidence can be established, then there is a possibility of exploring together the Bible passage and of hearing what God is saying to that group through the passage. Some of the material given in the first chapter of this book should be made known to the group. If they can learn of how groups of Christians in the Nazi period in Germany discovered the Bible to be a guide to life, if they know that the Confessing Church fought Nazism with the Word of God and won the battle, they will at least be prepared to discover for themselves that the Bible can speak to their generation. A democratic society in the West is no further removed from the society of biblical times than was the totalitarian society in Germany in the 'thirties. This cannot be overemphasized. Bible study requires some confidence in the Bible. This does not mean that no one should come to a Bible study group unless he has confidence in the Bible, but it does mean that the atmosphere of the group must be that of taking the Bible seriously and expecting to hear something. The group has met, not to discover what the Hebrews did with their pots and pans, but to learn what the message of the prophet is for them today in their society.

BRINGING THE BIBLE UP TO DATE

Given this confidence in the Bible, the group has then to discover how they can relate their Bible study to life. A group may be perfectly willing to accept the thesis that the Bible speaks today. It may even go so far as to believe that its main purpose in meeting is to hear what the Bible says to every member of the group in his society. But the question remains, How? Nearly all the books that we have and the pamphlets to help us understand the Bible tend to take us back into the society of those who wrote the various books of the Bible. A good deal of Bible study has consisted in going back. Men who have read the Bible all their lives know the geography of Palestine and the ways of the early Hebrews almost as well as they know their own landscape and the ways of their own people. There is some real importance in going back, because some of the things that are written in the Bible can only be understood in their setting. There are whole chapters of the Old Testament which are unintelligible unless we understand the conditions of the people at the time when they were written. But that is only the first step. The object of going back is to understand the words that are written. We have then started to answer the question, 'What did this mean?' No Bible study group can stop there. It must then ask the further question, 'What does this mean to us in our society?' This will require a considerable effort of mind. It will be almost like imagining Amos dressed in modern clothes. We must first of all know Amos in the eighth century BC. We must know something of the clothes he wore, of the conditions of life in his country, and of the dangers that beset the increase of luxury. Then we have to make a great effort of the imagination to bring Amos into twentieth century society and ask ourselves what he would say to our society if he were one of us. This effort is made in every good expository sermon, but there are very few good expository sermons. It was made supremely well by J. B. Phillips in his translation called *Letters to Young Churches*. The story of that translation is that he discovered the letters of the New Testament to be unintelligible to his people in London during the bombing. He was reading in church the Epistle to the Colossians. His people had been up all night during the air-raids and were beginning to fall asleep one by one as he read Paul's great sentences. It was not only that they were tired—the sentences meant nothing to them at all. J. B. Phillips went home and read his Greek again and asked himself why these letters meant so much to him and so little to his people. He discovered that it was because he could go back into the first century and his training had enabled him to understand what Paul was saying. He therefore set himself the task of translating the Greek of Paul's letter to the Colossians into an English which Paul would have used if he were speaking or writing to an English congregation in the twentieth century. That required an effort of the imagination as well as a quality of translation. A Bible study group has to go even further than J. B. Phillips went. It is not only concerned with translating the language of the Bible. It is concerned with translating the message of the Bible. This is no academic task; it is the task of a group of real people feeling the pressures of their own society in their lives and expecting from the Bible some word from God about their daily life. Many methods may be used. One is to imitate the method of the German pastors.

DIVISION OF TIME

An evening's Bible study can be divided into three parts. The first part can be a careful study of what the passage really means. This is when the material from the commentaries is reported, discussed and understood. This is when questions are asked about why some translators put one word and some put another in the same verse. This is where there can be an attempt made to get back into the mind and into the age of the early writers. The second part of the evening can be taken up with discussing the problems that are really in the minds of the people met together. It might even take the form of discussing the day's newspaper. This period must of course be limited in time or it will take up the whole evening. The third part of the evening can then be used for bringing the two discussions together. This will require very skilful leadership but it can be done with great success.

A much easier method, although perhaps not so fruitful, is to let the two worlds flow into one another naturally rather than attempt to bring them together logically. This is to follow something of the method of the Norwegian groups. The first part of the evening is a social one, and discussion is free and easy about the very things that are on the top of people's minds. The group comes together fresh from its experiences in the world and talks about the world. This discussion is encouraged, and then at a certain point Bible study begins. The leader can then refer back to some things which have been said in the early discussion whenever they seem to relate to something in the Bible passage studied. This is often a very successful way of ensuring that people do not leave their experiences outside when they come in to study the Bible. However it is done, the Bible study group must consciously make provision for relating the affairs of the world to the passage they are studying. Most Bible study groups will find that to do this they have to divide up the evening in one way or another.

THE WORD FOR LIVING

Once a group has discovered how to bring the concerns of the world into the group and relate them to Bible study, it has then to go one step further and bring what the members have learnt in Bible study to bear upon their life in the world afterwards. This is a great deal more difficult, and it may be a long time before the group is sufficiently experienced to do this deliberately. Of course it will be done incidentally; people who have attended Bible study groups for a long time and sought to understand what God is saying to them through the Bible will lead better lives in the world. Yet more can be done than simply allowing the Bible study to have its influence almost unconsciously. There can be a deliberate planning, and some groups have tried this with great success. When a Bible passage has been studied, and its meaning has been related to the contemporary world, it has then to be lived in the world. This Word of God must not only be something said to his people, it must also be the Word for living. Only a mature group can plan this with care. It can take several forms. People who know one another well because they have met together often, and who have confidence that the Bible is a book to be lived by, can covenant together to live by what they have learnt. When a passage deals, for example, with honesty, they may set themselves the task, after the Bible study group, to examine their own daily life to see whether the standards of honesty which they have approved in the Bible are the standards by which they are living. If they do this sensibly, they will also ask whether they should be the standards by which they should live in the world. Does a complicated industrial society involve a different kind of honesty?

The effort to live by what has been learnt will again affect the discussion of the Bible study group itself. Let us take the passage which has been quoted in so many versions earlier in this chapter. Here Simon has tried to buy a spiritual gift. He has been roundly rebuked, in a way that can leave no doubt about the apostle's disapproval. Indeed the rebuke contains more oaths than almost any rebuke in the Bible. Simon was well and truly told that what he was trying to do was a thoroughly wicked thing. The word 'simony' has entered into our vocabulary as a result of this passage. Any member of the group will see at once that 'trafficking in church preferment' is a bad thing. As the group will be entirely composed of laymen, they will be able to disapprove of clergy who try to get preferment by underhand means. Such is an unprofitable occupation for a Bible study group. They will soon begin to see that the passage applies equally well to lay people who try to buy influence. The man who is appointed a deacon in the church because he is supporting the church generously may well feel embarrassed as this chapter is being discussed. Any Bible study group will begin to apply this passage to the lives not only of the clergy they know but also of themselves. It would then be a good occupation for a group to keep this passage in mind during the next week and see how often they used their possessions or their position to get preferment, even in spiritual work.

That is a simple example of how a Bible passage might be lived in the coming week. The Bible study group is beginning to have a real effect when it does this. It is beginning to expose the lives of its members to the Word of God as it is heard in the passage studied. It would need to go further than simply doing this in the personal lives of its members. It should continue to influence the community life of the society in which the members live. There are many Bible study groups where careful Bible study has led members not only to live themselves in obedience to the Word of God but to take action which would make the society of which they are members more in conformity with the will of God. Such is effective Bible study.

PREPARATION

All these things that have been mentioned can be done in a Bible study group, but they will require the attention and the preparation of the members. The question of how much preparation and how much planning a Bible study group should have will soon become a big issue. It is as well to settle at the very beginning what is to be done. A Bible study group can become most unprofitable if every other week it is discussing its future. Some groups will wish to work their way through a book of the Bible. That can be a good method, provided the leader is well-equipped and is prepared to stop from time to time to consider issues that have arisen as the result of the study. Other groups will wish to follow a syllabus so that they get the teaching of the Bible on one particular subject. Other groups may even wish to follow the Christian Year and study the doctrines as they arise through the year, with special reference to the relevant Bible passages. Some strongly liturgical churches, particularly Lutherans, tend to favour this kind of Bible study. It has the advantage of rooting the Bible study in the orthodox doctrine of the Church.

STUDY OUTLINES

Whichever method is followed, there will be need sooner or later for a study outline. The minister of the church can provide this for the groups in his own church, or a denomination may print a large number of copies to be used over a wide area. The study outline will be needed. It is not to be a book of instructions which gives all the necessary answers to the appropriate questions, neither is it to be a series of questions which ought to be asked. It should help the leader, but most of all it should help the members of the group to direct their attention in preparation to the big issues raised by the passage. Many of these study outlines have been used in different countries.

AN EXAMPLE FROM SCOTLAND

Sometimes it is necessary for an outline to go into details if a specific subject is being studied as well as a passage from the Bible. This was the case in preparing for Scotland's second Kirk Week. It was decided to direct the attention of the churches in Scotland to the part played by suffering in developing a community life according to the Will of God. Passages were chosen and a simple study outline was circulated to the churches. It was later used by the seventy separate Bible study groups that met during the Kirk Week. For the leaders, a more detailed outline was prepared, including background information and detailed verse by verse comments. The following is a reproduction of the simpler study outline as used by all those at Kirk Week.

PREPARING FOR KIRK WEEK

The essence of Kirk Week is to find out what God is saying to the people of Scotland in this day and generation. There is no easy way to do this, and there are no clever leaders who know and want to tell you. The people of Scotland have to listen for themselves, and to help them do so, we have chosen certain passages from the Bible for careful study. They will be studied in many small groups at Kirk Week; but, long before that, people who may never come to Kirk Week will be reading these passages in all the churches. What they discover will be brought to Kirk Week by their representatives and will enrich the groups.

These notes are to help you do this. They contain no answer to questions. That is your job as you meet in Bible study, seeking to discover what God is saying to you in these portions of his Word.

These particular passages have been chosen because it seems that what we most want to know today is how we can live together. In family, in church, in our local community, in nation and among the nations, we find it much easier to be selfish, to develop our own personality, than to live with others as part of a fellowship.

These passages, from Exodus to 1 Peter, concern the problems of a community, God's laws and his promises, his judgment and his redemption, his love and his concern for a people in society. What the Bible says on these matters is important for us in the crisis of our time.

I. *Exodus* 19 *and* 20 : *An Ethical Basis for Society*

The things that men will do for their country they would be ashamed to do for themselves. This is a fact which poses problems at once. If religion is a private affair and men think of the Ten Commandments as guides to their personal life, they may still miss the real point of these two chapters. Here we have an account of God meeting with a people and laying down the basis of the kind of society he can honour. If we read the chapters in that way and look at the list of Commandments as basic requirements for a just society, we shall learn much about what God requires of our societies. This is not a new approach, by any means. When King Alfred was drawing up the laws for England in his famous document which became one of the bases of English law, he headed it with an Anglo-Saxon translation of several chapters from Exodus, including these two. Try to see what is required of our society in the light of these chapters. Read them through carefully and get the setting. If it will help to stimulate your imagination, go to see the film *The Ten Commandments* or read the two novels by Arthur E. Southon called *This Evil Generation* and *On Eagle's Wings*. It is good to get a rounded picture of Moses, the great leader and man of God.

Exodus 19. 1-2

The deliverance from Egypt had been a real thing. At the time, many must have had great ideas of the future; but the majority just wanted to throw off the Egyptian yoke. Here they all are now, 'encamped in the wilderness', much as we, or more especially an occupied people of Europe, felt in 1945. The deliverance was real. But now, what of the future?

vv. 3-6

God speaks to his man. Throughout this study, we shall have to ask ourselves who are the men to whom God has spoken in these years since the end of the war and whether we have heeded them. Here we have God's promise. Is it purely a matter of God and Israel or does it still have meaning for us today?

vv. 7-9a

Read this carefully in our setting. Moses comes from God, consults with the elders and then calls upon the people for an act of dedication. The authority of God is with him, but undoubtedly part of his authority for the people is that he has been the Liberator. The first requirement is the agreement of the people.

vv. 9b-15

There is much in this passage which belongs to its time; but essentially it still holds. If we are to meet with God, we must prepare ourselves. We shall need to do more than wash our clothes. Maybe the modern equivalent is 'to put out of our minds all that hinders'. Maybe we have to consider what our Lord said, 'First be reconciled to your brother' (Matt. 5. 24). Discuss what is required of a people today before they can approach God.

vv. 16-25

The awesome setting is not without importance. The details may seem a little primitive to us, but such a moment was not a time for familiarity with God. He is to give, with great authority not to be challenged or discussed, his terms for a just society. Much more will be needed, but in chapter 20 we are given the basic requirements. Before coming to the details of the separate commandments, discuss what authority they have for us today. It might be as well to discuss openly how far the Bible is still an authority. There have been many changes in our attitude to the Bible in the last fifty years. It has had its ups and downs. At present it seems to be having one of its ups; but we need more than a dependence upon the theological fashion to give us

confidence in the Bible. That confidence we need. We may
have many qualifications, but unless we have confidence in
the Bible we are not likely to hear God's Word to us
through it.

Exodus 20

Read the Ten Commandments one by one in a community
sense. Do you think these commandments would make
better 'wayside pulpits' than the usual pieces of good advice? Would they have any meaning apart from the personal?

v. 2

This identifies God and stakes his claim. Is there an equivalent? Can we say, 'This is the God you praised at Dunkirk'?
or, 'This is the God who gave greatness to your nation'? or
what?

v. 3

What 'other gods' can a nation have?

vv. 4-6

What is idolatry in a modern nation?

v. 7

Have we been guilty as a nation of taking God's name in
vain? e.g. Did we do so in time of war when we claimed
that our cause was his? Or do we do so in our correspond-
ence with Communists?

vv. 8-11

What does this mean in terms of Sabbath observance in

a modern society? Should our laws enforce it as they do other commandments? How can a nation keep a day holy?

v. 12

What does this mean in terms of our care for the aged among us? Does it mean also respect for the thought and ideals of a previous generation?

vv. 13-17

Take each of these commandments and ask similar questions. What constitutes killing, adultery, stealing, false witness, covetousness? Don't assume you know. These words have a wider meaning than we sometimes think. Read Matt. 5.17-48 to see how Jesus adapts them for his day. Then try to do the same for a community life today.

vv. 18-26

This sounds very primitive, but read it carefully and see if there is anything here which helps us to understand our own relations with God, our worship and our approach to God as a nation. What do we mean by fearing God today? Is there still something in

> 'Fear him, ye saints, and you will then
> Have nothing else to fear.'

II. *Amos* 1 *and* 2 : *Condemnation of an Unjust Society*

Amos is the first of the 'writing prophets'. He addressed the same nation as Moses led out of Egypt and he could assume the acceptance of the Ten Commandments as a basis. He lived some eight centuries before Christ and he was a man up from the country, with a dislike of city life. The people were now settled in the land and they already had a history. They were prosperous, and it seemed to Amos that this had done them no good. He longed for the simple religion of the wilderness. There was no doubt that the simple religion had got a bit mixed up with Canaanite religions, and prosperity had brought luxury, class oppression and sin. There were two nations: Judah in the south, clustered around Jerusalem; Israel in the north, with its capital in rich, sinful Samaria. The two great powers were Assyria and Egypt and the two little kingdoms of Israel and Judah lay on a bridge between them. It was obvious to Amos that sooner or later one or both of the kingdoms would be destroyed by one or both of the two great powers. He called on the kingdoms to be just and called on God to defend them. He poured condemnation on the surrounding nations also. His great contemporary, Isaiah, constantly told Judah not to ally herself with anyone, lest she be destroyed. Amos was not so politically minded as Isaiah, although he approved of this advice to Israel also. For him foreign alliances were not so much politically dangerous as morally dangerous. He saw a grim future for sinful Israel.

Amos 1.1

Here is the setting and the date. Amos was later silenced and presumably returned to Tekoa. This reads as though he or one of his followers wrote down his words, carefully dated, 'two years before the earthquake', as a testimony when the time should come that he told them so!

v. 2

Here is the setting of Sinai again. When God speaks it is no light thing.

vv. 3-5

Inhumanity in war will be judged. Damascus is the capital of Syria.

vv. 6-8

Can we read of Gaza's terrible act without remembering our own decision to depopulate the eastern provinces of Germany in 1945 and send ten million into exile? The Philistines, now holding the coastal cities only, are to be judged.

vv. 9-10

Tyre is singled out for a similar cruelty.

vv. 11-12

Edom has already appeared. Again, inhumanity in war.

vv. 13-15

Ammon is condemned for aggression.

Amos 2.1-3

Moab is condemned for desecration.

Up to this point, the condemnation would sound like the condemnation of Belsen and Buchenwald by a Scottish prophet. All the hearers of Amos rejoiced. If now he turned to England we should begin to get a little uncomfortable. It is just that which Amos does when he turns to Judah.

vv. 4-5

Judah's condemnation seems a little tame after the atrocities of the others; but it is not shown to be less serious. They have moved away from God's laws. They have re-

jected the basis on which God made them a nation. Therefore, they will be reduced to defencelessness.

Is the careless failure to keep God's laws as serious a
matter as the deliberate cruelty of inhumanity in war, atrocities in concentration camps? Should England's rejection of
God be judged as harshly as Nazi Germany's arrogance or
Communist Russia's atheism?

Amos now turns to Israel—his hearers.

vv. 6-8

Israel's transgressions are spelled out in detail. There is no
justice in the courts, no pity in common life, no decency
in the home, no piety in worship. In these verses there are
illustrations of the breaking of specific commandments,
such as the garment taken in pledge (v. 8) and sins which
break the accepted sense of decency even within immoral-
ity, such as father and son taking the same woman (v. 7).
What list would Amos make for Scotland?

vv. 9-11

A recital of what God has done. Can we recall what God
has done for Scotland? Could the same confident claim be
made at the end of it, 'Is it not indeed so, O people of
Israel?' (RSV).

v. 12

In particular, God has sent his warnings and the people
have corrupted his men. How far does this apply to us? A
young preacher, full of the Spirit of God, can be handled
so that he soon ceases to say what the people do not like.
What is our equivalent to giving the Nazirites wine to
drink?

vv. 13-16

Israel's punishment. A people defeated. Ponder these verses well. How do we understand them? Is it that Israel's real strength was in her God and, now that she has rejected God, God withdraws himself from her and her strength departs? How then will God deal with us?

III. *Isaiah: A Society Redeemed by Suffering*

The passages chosen from Isaiah are what are usually known as the Servant Songs. They have been applied, particularly Isaiah 53, to the suffering and mission of our Lord, and there is some evidence that he so applied them himself. We do not need to dispute that they are prophecies of Christ because the spirit of these passages is perfectly fulfilled in him. Yet they have a more immediate application to the role of a community and it is in this sense that they can be studied most profitably.

(a) *Isaiah 42. 1-7*

The passage is divided into two parts: vv. 1-4, the true picture of a nation as God's servant leading the other nations of the world to the light; and vv. 5-7, God's vindication of his servant. If you glance a little further on at v. 9 you will see that this is not a picture of what is happening, but of what God desires.

vv. 1-4

Our ideas of a dominant nation have not changed much since Isaiah's day: it is still a nation with enough power to enforce its will. These verses give us a quite different picture. God's spirit does not give 'might'; it gives gentleness, power to suffer without crying out for help, faithfulness seeking justice for all, patience and hope to the end.

Read these verses carefully and see whether it is possible for a nation to regard them as the great qualities? Is this what we mean when we talk of Britain's new role as that of 'moral leadership'?

vv. 5-7

The change is now to triumph. True moral leadership seems to be a calling from God, inspired by him and led by him. Where is the nation able to accept this role? Certainly Israel failed. Read v. 19 and ask how far this could be applied to the Church.

(b) *Isaiah* 49. 1-13

This is a beautiful poem that needs reading right through before discussion begins. It tells of Israel's call. That call is not only for the sake of Israel, but for the whole world (see v. 6). All the nations of the world are to be blessed in Israel's faithfulness and her example. She is to be 'a light to the nations' and God's salvation is to reach 'to the end of the earth'. It would be well to read this section, especially v. 6, in the Revised Standard Version or some modern translation. This passage is appropriate to the Church's spiritual possessions. They are not for the enjoyment of 'church members only'. God's servant, whether it be Israel or the Church of Christ, is for the nations. Discuss how this applies in Scotland. What is the attitude of the Church to those outside? 'Where is the boasting? It is excluded.'

(c) *Isaiah* 50. 4-9

Read and ponder. This is what it means to be God's servant.

Many a faithful Christian has discovered this in a concentration camp. Many a Jew remembered this in Nazi Germany. Suffering does not lead to bitterness or hatred of the persecutor. It would help to understand this passage if the group would acquaint itself with some modern story of heroism and faithfulness under persecution.[1] A society can be redeemed by a suffering Church. Is it possible that a suffering nation could thus serve the world? Discuss what part suffering plays today in the Church—here in Scotland. Has there been any call to suffer which we have refused to hear? It is not usual to include the two following verses (vv. 10 and 11) as part of the Servant Song; but they are a good comment on those who reject God's call to be his servant and walk in his way:

> Who among you fears the Lord
>   and obeys the voice of his servant,
> who walks in darkness
>   and has no light,
> yet trusts in the name of the Lord
>   and relies upon his God?
>
> Behold, all you who kindle a fire,
>   who set brands alight!
> Walk by the light of your fire,
>   and by the brands which you have kindled!
> This shall you have from my hand:
>   you shall lie down in torment.

(d) *Isaiah* 52. 13-53.9

It is extremely difficult to think of this famous fifty-third chapter without thinking of the Passion of our Lord. We still hear Handel's lovely aria 'He was despised and rejected',

---

[1] E.g. the present writer's *Paul Schneider: The Pastor of Buchenwald*, SCM Press, 1956.

and we see the lonely, regal figure buffeted by the soldiery. All this is legitimate; but once the chapter had meaning before Christ came. That meaning we should try to recover. Read it afresh, beginning in chapter 52 at verse 13, and try to hear it as addressed to a people—Israel—called to suffer. Can the Church see itself as called to the same humiliation? The fifty-third chapter is the bridge between the Servant Songs and the Passion of our Lord. It helps us to see how Israel's destiny was fulfilled, narrowed down into the person of Christ and continued in the Christian Church as the body of Christ. That is not the whole story, because Israel has continued to play her part in history, suffering and redeeming. Yet, for us the line is clear. This passage is fulfilled in Christ and is to be fulfilled in the Church. What part does suffering play today in the Church?

IV. *John* 18: *The Passion of the Son of God*

To move from Isaiah 53 to John 18 is to move without a break. We are still in the same circle of ideas, but now poetry has become hard historical reality. Suffering is at the heart of our religion. It is now demonstrated in the suffering of our Lord. The chapter has to be read slowly, and pondered section by section until we recognize ourselves there, at least as spectators.

vv. 1-9

Here is the story of betrayal and arrest. The voluntary isolation of the Son of God. He is taking the suffering upon himself. 'Let these men go.' We must enquire whether this has a wider meaning. Jesus and his disciples are together involved. In the eyes of those who arrested Jesus, the whole band is dangerous. Jesus steps forward and buys their release with his own suffering. More than once in this chapter John hints at a wider meaning. Can we find it here?

vv. 10-11

A useless act, but one for which we are all grateful to Peter. It was the natural, primitive response of a friend. Yet Jesus uses it to show how useless it is to defend with weapons the Son of God. Can we say the same of the Church of Christ? Is it better to be destroyed than to strike a blow?

vv. 12-14

The arrest is made. Note the wide application of Caiaphas's remark. What does it mean to us? How can Christ die 'for us'?

vv. 15-18

The beginning of Peter's denial. The defender of the Christ is a sorry picture now. Yet he tried to follow.

vv. 19-24

The trial. Jesus does not really defend himself.

vv. 25-27

The denial is complete and the cock crows. The behaviour of Peter is well worth studying and sobers any assurance we have that in the hour of trial we shall remain firm.

vv. 28-32

The shifting of responsibility is pathetically human. How often have we allowed others to do what we could have prevented? We all hesitate to soil our hands. Yet Pilate and Caiaphas are equally guilty.

vv. 33-38

Read carefully. Is Jesus evading the questions or answering them at a profounder level than they are being asked?

vv. 39-40

Pilate lets the mob decide. Yet he cannot evade the responsibility. He is only remembered for this—'Crucified under Pontius Pilate.'

This chapter can only be studied in prayer; but we can see in it the link between the Old Testament and the New Testament. We need to ask what it has to do with a community. Is it a purely personal chapter or does it affect the way men live together? How far is the mob guilty? How far did the disciples fail? If the Church is the body of Christ, do we feel in our life the effect of his Passion? That Christ has suffered 'once and for all' may lead to the conclusion that the Church need not suffer. Is this true? What relation have the sufferings of the Church to the sufferings of Christ?

V. 1 Peter 4 and 5 : The Christian Community in the World

There is an immediate connection between this and the last passage. The persecution which had already broken over the young Christian Church is seen as linked with the sufferings of Christ. The martyr has a closeness to Christ especially in his suffering, which lifts him above the world. Suffering liberates him. It must be remembered in reading these two chapters that Peter is writing under the stress of persecution and the expectation of a speedy end to the world. He therefore calls upon his fellow Christians to separate themselves from the world's pleasures. His exhortation is to the Christian community, but at the same time he gives instruction about living in society which has direct application to our own problems. We must not forget the difference in setting, but neither must we abandon the passage as irrelevant.

1 *Peter* 4. 1-6

The connection with Christ's suffering should be discussed. How can the suffering of a Christian for his faith help the society in which he lives? This passage suggests a firm separation between pagan society and the Christian community. Has it any relevance for Scotland, which is nominally Christian?

vv. 7-11

We do not all feel the sense of urgency that Peter feels. The end of the world did not come; but is there an abiding urgency? Do the instructions for holy living apply equally when we do not expect the sudden breaking in of the judgment day?

vv. 12-19

At this point it looks as though news has just reached Peter that a new wave of persecution had broken out. Perhaps this was the beginning of the Neronian persecution. 'Fiery ordeal' suggests this. Again he calls upon them to rejoice at suffering, because it brings a Christian into closer fellowship with the suffering of his Lord. However, he makes a distinction. The suffering must be blameless. If it is our own fault, we dare not compare it with Christ's. The man who loses his job because he is a bad workman must not talk of being discriminated against because he is a Christian. Discuss the relevance of this today. Peter is saying, 'Live a good life, and then if you suffer, not because you are making a nuisance of yourself but because you are a Christian, rejoice.' It is a very serious thing for a Christian to defy the law. Discuss this in the light of Christians living today in Communist countries. Should we expect them to defy the law? When and why should they act unlawfully?

1 *Peter* 5

Here is detailed instruction for living, well worth careful study. Much of it concerns personal relations which are the web of society.

vv. 1-5

The elders and the youth. Read these verses very carefully in the light of relations between church members. The motives are carefully stressed. You have seen Christ suffer, you are partakers of the glory, therefore. . . . Can we say that our care for young people in our church or in our community is done from such high motives? Note also the manner, not 'domineering'. Young people also are called upon to clothe themselves with humility. This is a practical section.

vv. 6-11

Here is a general passage calling for faithfulness and endurance. Can we measure our life today in the light of this exhortation to a suffering church?

vv. 12-24

The greetings.

Epilogue

It will now be time to look back at the five areas chosen and see whether a simple pattern has emerged. What is God saying to us through these very different passages? The motive is one thing. Why are we asked to write a prohibition of killing into the constitution of a just society? Is it for humanitarian reasons? Why is an elder asked to deal gently with a young man? The depth of motive should now be discussed. Many of the passages have also raised the question of the purpose of suffering. Through Moses, Amos, Isaiah, John and Peter, God is speaking to us in our day and generation.

What does he say?

ANOTHER EXAMPLE—FROM AMSTERDAM

A quite different kind of study outline was needed for certain small groups in Amsterdam. They had been formed as the result of a need for fellowship in the big town. The groups belonged to a very narrow Calvinistic Church in Holland and therefore their approach to the Bible was rather different from that used in Scotland's Kirk Week, although both the Church of Scotland and the Church in Amsterdam are Presbyterian. The following is a specimen study outline which proved successful with this kind of group in Amsterdam.

Ephesians 4. 25-32

Notice that throughout this passage there are two ideas, 'putting off' and 'putting on'. In the preceding verses, we had been told that we must 'put off our old nature' (v. 22) and 'put on the new nature' (v. 24). In another letter, Paul said we must 'put on the Lord Jesus' (Rom. 13.14). How can Paul speak of these things so easily? The 'old nature' is not a jacket to be taken off. Paul himself found it difficult, as he says in Romans 7.

This passage, beginning with Eph. 4.25, begins to speak in practical terms. The two ideas are related to everyday activities. However, embedded in the series of practical exhortations are two terms which seem out of place : the devil (v. 27), the Holy Spirit (v. 30). Paul clearly did not separate practical things from spiritual language. This whole passage ends with Christ and his grace (v. 32), just as the preliminary verses dealt with him (v. 20, 21). This passage deals with the good life, only in relation to Christ and lived by his grace. Now for some verse by verse comments.

v. 25

'Putting away falsehood' and 'speaking the truth'. Is there a difference between these two? First, consider why a man tells lies. Is it fear of punishment, shame, greed, need to keep up a pretence of goodness, need to exaggerate the faults of others? Can you think of other reasons? Paul gives his reason for 'putting away falsehood'. He says, 'for we are members one of another'. Does this mean that lying always indicates a deficiency of love? Is 'speaking the truth', in the full sense, only possible when there is love? In this connection, discuss lying which is not intended to hurt, but rather the opposite. What do you think of flattery? Consider how seldom, even in marriage, we dare tell the whole truth to anyone. Is it because we do not wish to hurt or is it because of lack of true love or even because of cowardice? Discuss in particular, how we should 'speak the truth' among our fellow church members.

84

v. 26

This deals with anger. There are two kinds of anger : anger because someone has injured me, anger against sin. The latter could be called 'righteous indignation' and is a reflection of God's anger against sin. Here, Paul is concerned with the other kind of anger. Yet, he seems to approve. 'Be angry.' What does that mean? Is anger really permitted? What about the qualification 'but do not sin'? What is it that contains the anger so that it does not surge up and lead to sin? Why should the sun not go down on one's anger? Control of anger can be discussed profitably.

v. 27

Now we come to the text about 'the devil'. Why is it here, in this setting? What does he mean by 'give opportunity'? An old proverb may throw some light on this verse : 'When summer comes, you can't stop the birds from flying into your house; but you can stop them from building their nests there!' Does that fit the teaching of this verse? Discuss some examples from elsewhere in the Bible which illustrate 'giving opportunity to the devil'. Ask whether there are examples also in your own life.

v. 28

Notice the lovely contrast between 'stealing' and 'giving'. There is nothing here about the opposite of stealing, only about keeping for oneself. Why not? How then should we regard all our earthly possessions? We can notice here how Paul sees love as behind the whole of life, the only thing which can really make our lives new.

v. 29

This deals with our speaking—in company, at parties and on other occasions. Paul reminds us that God is also there. What does a 'good' word mean here? And why is this further defined as 'for edifying'? Here, Jesus comes to our parties. What does he say of our conversations and what part will he take in them? Can an ordinary conversation over ordinary things be 'such as is good'? Or must it always be a serious conversation? This verse suggests two criteria of judgment: 'edifying' and 'impart grace'. Can you recall a conversation, not about 'godly' things, which could be said to 'edify'? What does the word 'grace' mean in this context?

v. 30

Now we come to the text about 'the Holy Spirit'. Why is it here, in this setting? Is there a connection with the previous verses? It is of very great importance to grasp the full meaning of 'grieve' in this verse. Compare it with 'blasphemy against the Spirit' (Matt. 12.31), 'to lie to the Holy Spirit' (Acts 5.3), 'quench the Spirit' (1 Thess. 5.19). Can a child of God ever 'grieve' the Holy Spirit? Do you know examples? Perhaps, when I do not allow him to work in me.

For the phrase, 'in whom you were sealed' compare Eph. 1.13. What does this mean, that the Spirit is given to us when we are sealed? What does God give to us in our 'sealing' and what has it to do with this verse? Does it make our grieving of the Holy Spirit more serious?

vv. 31-32

The two verses belong together. Again, we are told what

to take off (or put away) and what to put on. 'Bitterness', what is that? 'Wrath and anger', the two lie close together. 'Clamour and slander' are the consequences of sinful anger. 'Malice and guile' (cf. 1 Peter 2.1) is what destroys our life together as men. At the root of this lies a deeply ingrained egoism, by which each man thinks first and foremost of himself.

Opposed to this, Paul now takes a series of virtues, which can blossom wherever there is life together with Christ. 'Kind', i.e. we have nothing to seek for ourselves, not feverishly thinking on our own wants, because we know that God thinks of us and has thought of us in Christ Jesus and that we await the coming of God's glorious kingdom. From this peace, rest and confidence, a man can be friendly, 'kind'. Is there a difference between this deep-rooted 'friendliness' and our common use of the term? 'Tenderhearted' refers to the need of others. First, we must see the need. Discuss whether we do or do not often see the need of others. 'Forgiving one another'. Now, rightly, we come, by one means or another, to the Cross. That commits us at the end. What is the teaching of Jesus? Recall the parable in which Jesus says that the forgiveness we receive from God is dependent upon our forgiving others.

Now read the whole passage once more. Much is touched upon and much is also passed over. Can we now answer the question in our own lives—What is there that I must 'take off' and what must I 'put on'?

BASIC PRINCIPLES AGAIN

These two examples of study illustrate well the basic principles which were defined at the end of the first chapter. Although they are quite different in approach and in the theological assumptions they make, they are (1) at considerable depth, (2) related to the situation in which the people find themselves, however limited this may be, and (3) group studies. What this means is that both kinds of preparation have taken into account the serious difficulties inherent in reading the Bible. They have both been prepared by men who have taken the trouble to understand those difficulties and to analyse the background situation out of which the writings were prepared. It means also that both study outlines have taken into account the situation, in the one case in Scotland and in the other case in over-crowded Amsterdam. The first study outline is constantly referring the group to questions about the meaning of certain commands for Scotland in the mid-twentieth century. The second is much more pietistic in tendency, but none the less relates the Bible study to the conditions of loneliness which beset young people coming from the country and finding work in the big city. Finally, while both of them could be used in private study, they are designed for groups and will produce the best results when used in groups. Both assume that a group of Christians meeting together around the Bible and guided in the asking of their questions will discover something new. There is a certain excitement about the study in both forms of outline.

3

BIBLE STUDY GROUPS IN ACTION

IN this chapter I want to give the script of three different kinds of Bible study. They are not to be imitated, because any imitation of a discussion becomes artificial, but they may be read as examples of what really happens. They are all taken from real Bible study.

The first is a group of German professors preparing to lead the Bible study at the Frankfurt *Kirchentag*. This is more or less what happened in the discussion as they prepared with great detail what the selected passages were saying to Germany at that time—the time was 1956. The second is a series of Bible studies prepared for Yeovil Bible Week. Again, those taking part in the discussion were ministers. The text quoted was boiled down from a day's session and used in the separate congregations. The third is an ordinary Bible study group attempting to wrestle with a difficult chapter in the book of Hosea.

PREPARING FOR THE GERMAN KIRCHENTAG

The theme of the whole assembly is 'Reconciliation', and the text 'Be ye reconciled to God'. The three passages chosen for the basic Bible study are Luke 22. 7-20; 15. 11-32; Matt. 18. 21-35. These were thoroughly discussed at Arnoldshain in May by a small group of those who would lead the mass Bible study at the *Kirchentag*. In this summary of the general discussion it will be noticed that reconciliation remained the dominant theme and was seen in a spiritual sense.

1. *Luke* 22. 7-20

This is the passage dealing with the preparation for the Feast of Unleavened Bread, when Jesus longed to eat the Passover with his disciples. It tells of the secret arrangement with the man carrying the pitcher, and of the words of institution.

A good deal of work has been done upon the comparison and contrast between Luke and the other Gospels. Many questions have also been asked about what actual feast this was that Jesus celebrated with his disciples. There is some divergency within the New Testament itself. The point that concerns us, however, is the strong link that this incident has with the Passover. It cannot be understood without reference back to the Passover. There the people of God were throwing off the slavery of Egypt and were beginning their pilgrimage, and they were saved from the angel of death. The symbol and the power of this salvation was in the lamb slain, whose blood was sprinkled over the doorway. These men who met together for the Last Supper were Jews, and the story of the Exodus was their greatest story. They never forgot how God had brought them up out of Egypt, and that very phrase meant for them rescue from darkness and from sin and from death. The Passover was for them the great feast of deliverance, and now in the very shadow of it they meet with their master and hear words which are deliberately based upon the story of the Passover: the lamb slain, the blood sprinkled, the meal eaten together before they go out on pilgrimage. With their minds alerted in this way, Jesus speaks of his blood being spilled and of his body being broken. He talks also in v. 16 of fulfilment: 'I shall not eat it until it is fulfilled in the kingdom of God.' There is a double meaning here. The Passover is fulfilled. It is fulfilled in Christ in the very simple way that this meal they are eating is the final meaning of the Passover. It is not yet fulfilled, or rather not yet completed, in that it waits for the end of time when the kingdom shall come in glory. The Church thus lives always in the sense of this waiting for the great fulfilment, but it lives also on the strength of the fact that the Passover has been fulfilled in Christ.

When he hands to them the bread and the wine, and comments upon it, he reminds us of our representation by Christ. In this passage we can never get away from that representation: we are all in a sense like Barabbas, the man who should have died that day. Christ remains for ever, in Bonhoeffer's phrase, 'The man for others'. And yet —and this Paul was also to develop later—he is so uniting us with him that we die with him as part of his body. Here again is a double meaning. He takes our place, and yet in his suffering, in his death, we share. Otherwise what does 'buried with Christ in baptism' mean? To take the phrase 'the body of Christ' to mean the Church is to take the whole of Christ and not just some incident in his life, or his final glory. If we are his body, then we suffer with him and die with him and are buried with him, that we may rise with him in glory.

The men around the table at the Last Supper were men brought up in their Old Testament, and from the very beginning the Church saw the death of Christ and the Last Supper as linked with two passages in the Old Testament.

There was the cult, or worship, linked with the Passover, and there was the individual emphasis linked with Isaiah 53, the Suffering Servant. It is wrong to see one of these meanings developing out of the other—they were both there from the beginning. At the Lord's Table we are both joining in the act of the community as symbolic and as powerful as the Passover, and we are alone with God, remembering the suffering of his Servant. When he says, in v. 19, 'Do this in remembrance of me,' he is asking that we shall do more than eat and drink in a fashion reminiscent of the Last Supper: he is doing more than instituting the Communion Service or the Mass. He is asking that we proclaim, as at that moment he was proclaiming, the gospel of reconciliation. We Protestants have so remembered the preaching that we have neglected the sacraments, and one of the things that this passage says to us is that both are necessary, and only by both do we obey his injunction, 'Do this in remembrance of me.'

At Frankfurt/Main, when the people gather to study these Bible passages, and they begin with this one about the Last Supper, they will expect us to talk about our own Communion Service. As this passage receives its important position as the opening passage of the conference, their question will be 'Why?' They will understand if we choose the story of the death of Christ, because that is central, but among us we have celebrated the Communion Service so seldom that anyone who tries to put it centrally in German Protestant life or to celebrate it frequently will meet with resistance from those who say 'Why so often?' There is a hard question of Church practice and custom which will meet us right at the beginning. But we must not allow this passage to lead us into an argument about how often we

92

should celebrate the Communion Service. The great theme of the conference is 'Reconciliation'. 'We speak of him and not of ourselves.' When we do that we see some of the awful implications of this passage. It lights up that strange phrase, which is almost too terrible for us to accept : 'Christ became sin.' The whole teaching of this passage, as indeed that of the Passover as we look back on it, and perhaps also of Isaiah 53, is that reconciliation between God and man is not easily accomplished. There is no reconciliation without blood. There will be many who will ask quite simply, 'What kind of a God is this who requires such terrible judgment on his own Son before he can be reconciled?' As we listen to this question, we must remember that it is not God, a reluctant God, who has to be reconciled; but we who are reconciled to him. It is God who acts, God who comes out and makes the reconciliation possible, and it is not something which he is doing to his Son, 'God was in Christ reconciling himself unto himself.'

In one sense the Frankfurt *Kirchentag* takes up the Bible study where it was left four years ago at Stuttgart. There the great theme was 'The Exodus'; there in the midst of our refugee problem we discovered that their situation in the days of Moses was our situation too, and we turned gladly to the Bible to see what God says to us in that condition. Now we take up the theme again. What he said to us as we identified ourselves with his people of long ago, wandering through the desert in search of the promised land, becomes a powerful word to us now as we see that Passover which began the Exodus fulfilled in Christ, and as we recognized ourselves as going out on a new pilgrimage into the world, with a new power behind us, waiting complete fulfilment, or perhaps marching towards the complete fulfilment, when at the end of time his kingdom shall come in glory.

2. Luke 15. 11-32

This parable is so well known that you need to stand back from it a bit in order to see anything new. One way is to compare it with another parable in the Gospels about two sons, the parable in Matt. 21. 28-32. That is of a father who had two sons and asked them each to go to work in his vineyard. One refused but later went and worked; the other said Yes, but did nothing. That parable contains the same relation of father to son as the parable we are studying, but does not raise the issue of the relation between the two brothers. It is this relation which is new in the parable and to which we must pay special attention. But first the relation of the son to the father.

The younger son is usually meant when we talk about the prodigal son and we might well ask where the younger son's sin begins. Schlatter says that it begins when he asks for his possessions: it is a sin of self-sufficiency, he is not content to be under the father's law and constraint any longer. He leaves the father's house in rebellion. But this is not a very satisfactory explanation. At that time, when Jesus told the parable, there were nearly five million Jews in the world and only half a million of them lived in Palestine. Far and away the larger number of Jews lived in the diaspora. It must therefore have been quite usual for a son to go to his father and ask for his inheritance that he might go and make a life himself. The elder brother would then remain at home to inherit the farm. The scene therefore which Jesus depicts is one that must have happened many times and there is nothing extraordinary in it.

94

The sin of the younger brother is that he wasted his substance and also in the way that he did it. This is depicted
clearly, and the downfall of the young man could not be
told in fewer words or more vividly. When he comes to
himself, however, he is clearer-sighted in the recognition of
his sin and also of his new status in relation to his father.
He not only renounces the right to be a son but he drops
two stages : he asks that he might be a hired servant, which
is one stage lower than a servant. Of this parable Bultmann
says quite simply 'It tells of God's love. The father is God,
the sons are his children, rebellious or obedient, forgiving
or unforgiving. It is an allegory of God's relation with men.'
Jeremias however wishes to preserve the form of a parable,
and therefore says this parable is simply a picture of a
father's love.[1] It shows how a father does behave towards
his son and then draws the conclusion : God is like that.
It is in that sense the same type of saying as 'If you then
who are evil, know how to give good gifts to your children,
how much more will your Father . . . ?' One of the first
questions raised by this parable is 'Are we dealing with a
parable or with an allegory?' Has it one clear meaning
directed against the Pharisees and those who are like them,
or has it many points which we can detect as we read
through the parable and which we can apply to our own
relation with God?

The parable is so human and given in such detail that it
is at least attractive to take it more in the nature of an
allegory than a parable. At least we can detect many of the
details of this parable in our dealing one with another.
Young men who have returned from long imprisonment in
Russia have known something of this return of the prodigal;

[1] See *The Parables of Jesus*, Eng. trs. 1954, pp. 105 f.

the restoration between the father and the son has been re-enacted a thousand times on a shattered German railway station. Many a young man has just come forward saying 'Father', and at that moment both have understood better than ever before what the father and the younger son felt when they met on the road. Yet we must not be sentimental in interpreting this parable. Some who have come in from the Eastern Zone and seen the prosperity of Western Germany have made the very strong comment, 'Do we know that we have lost a war and we were guilty?' The same difficulty arises in the Eastern Zone where one is so preoccupied with the problem of living under a Communist government that it is easy to forget the guilt of past years. This young son did not do that. He did not let the reception completely silence his confession of guilt. Yet sometimes as we read the story we feel this young man got let off much too lightly: it was hardly fair to the older brother. That needs pondering from the point of view of the younger brother. It is easy to apply this parable to the self-righteous, as indeed it was first applied to the Pharisees in our Lord's day, but we must not forget that many of us are really in the position of this prodigal, having wasted our substance, returning to God empty-handed. The story is not finished, we are not told whether the elder son went in to be reconciled with his brother or not. That open ending, leaving the father facing the elder son and saying to him, 'Your brother is here; come in,' leaves us with the central problem of the parable. It is really about reconciliation of God and the soul. Yet the story is too simple. Where is the Cross in this forgiveness? Luther never preached from the parable of the prodigal son. His comment was 'There is no son in this parable, only the father.' He saw it almost as a pre-

Christian parable. The question still needs to be asked: Where is the Cross and the sacrifice and the suffering in this parable? The prodigal returns home and is forgiven; the only problem seems to lie in reconciling the elder brother. It simply says, 'God is love,' and that, without the background of Christian understanding, may be a non-Christian comment. It underestimates the separation of a man from God when he has sinned. Yet others have noticed that the sin is there all right, and the Cross, in the price that the father paid.

The last verse of the parable also contains a reference to the Resurrection and the effect of the Cross; here we are told of the younger brother being dead and coming to life, being lost and found. That is an early and simple statement of 'Risen with Christ'. Whether or not it was intended in the original parable, it was certainly intended in the recounting of it. The central message of the parable however is in the father, who goes out to both sons. The prodigal son is not expected to find his way home alone; neither is the elder brother able to find his way back to fellowship with his brother alone. God comes out to both. And perhaps that is the central message of this parable for the *Kirchentag*. It is that whether we are like the younger son, having wasted our substance, or like the older son, hard and unforgiving, needing reconciliation with our brother, God comes out to meet us and to effect in us that which is necessary. He receives the younger son and restores him to sonship. He receives the elder son and restores him, or at least tries to restore him, to the status of a brother. The difference between these two sons and their response to the father coming out is that which makes the parable so pointed. It is, in some ways, easier for the younger son to accept forgiveness and be reconciled with his father, than it is for the elder brother. It is noticeable that the younger brother says 'Father' as his first word, but the older has instead a complaint: he does not say 'Father'. Surely this reminds us that when our relation with our brother is broken, then our relation with God is also seriously disturbed. 'He who does not love his brother whom he has seen, cannot love God whom he has not seen.' That is a fair comment on the parable.

At Frankfurt this passage will most certainly declare that God comes out to meet us: the obedient and the proud.

3. *Matthew* 18. 21-35

This is a parable dealing with a very practical issue which Peter had raised. Peter asks how long he has to go on forgiving his brother if he perpetually sins against him. Peter makes a generous gesture of seven times, and is told that that is not enough. In effect he is told he must always forgive, even if he knows that his brother is an habitual sinner. The reason is given in the parable: God has forgiven us far more than we are ever asked to forgive our brother. The parable goes further: it says that unless we do forgive our brother we are in no state in which God can forgive us. This is the parable of the unforgiving servant. It is well known. It illustrates what a great East European thinker called 'solidarity of guilt'. There is no guilt in the world in which we do not, in some measure, share. An unforgiving attitude disturbs the whole complex of relations between man and man, and man and God. Forgiveness is a healthy and proper reaction to a sin against us—forgiveness because we have been forgiven. Not to forgive is to insist upon remaining in the slave-to-slave relationship with our brother.

It is well known that the conditions of slavery tend to encourage an attitude between slaves which is of a low moral order. What this parable does is to show the kind of thing happening that might well have happened among a community of slaves.

The king freely forgives, and that is a kingly gesture; but the slave exacts all he possibly can from his fellow-slave, and that is a slavish gesture. As we read the story, we can so easily forget the difference between the slave mentality and the king mentality. We might ask, 'Why did this man going out from the king's presence, having had the great load of guilt lifted from him, behave in this way?' His behaviour certainly shows that the forgiveness had not altered the man : it had left him just where he was, with the mind of a slave. There is one little point that may be missed on first reading : when the slave who owed so much begged forgiveness of the king, he asked for time to pay and said that he would then pay all. The forgiveness may have cancelled the debt; but the words are a little ambiguous, and it may mean that he simply got what he asked for, namely, time to pay. If that were so, it was the most natural thing for him to try to collect his debts, and gather together every penny that he could to pay the debt. What he forgot, even if this were true, was that the other slave was precisely in the position that he had been in when he begged forgiveness of the king.

There is a very human touch in this story in the attitude of the other slaves. They at least had retained some kind of human relation. They were moved by the ill-treatment of their fellow-slave. Out of compassion for the one who was to be condemned for his debt, they went to the king and complained. What the king had failed to do by his forgiveness was now regarded as impossible, and the first slave was thrown into prison. The parable is not only an answer to Peter's question; it is also a study of the effect of forgiveness. Forgiveness had not changed the man. What the king was trying to do in the parable is what God is doing to us all the time. In our human nature we tend to behave as one slave to another. We seek ruin. God is seeking to lift up that relation until it is on a higher level : the relation of brothers who belong to the one family in which he is father.

This interpretation of the story helps us to explain its strange ending, which seems to make forgiveness by God dependent upon our forgiveness of one another. That dependence is put again in the Lord's Prayer : 'Forgive us our trespasses as we forgive them that trespass against us.' There are several passages of the New Testament like that. They are hard and difficult. Not many of us like to have God deal with us in the same way as we deal with other people. Yet this parable shows the whole complex of relations which may make forgiveness impossible. It is simplified in the parable : the king is disappointed with the slave whom he had forgiven because he did not go out and forgive. He had failed to raise him to the level of a king in his actions. In actual life, and it is that which the Bible is mirroring, forgiveness may raise a man. If it does not, then it has largely failed. The true forgiveness of God is that which changes a man's relation with his brother on to a higher level. So the parable comes full circle back to Peter. Unless it is natural for you now to forgive and forgive and forgive, then the forgiveness of God has been ineffective in you.

What tremendous lessons there are here for us in our day, in the relation between men who were once at war, men who were guilty, East and West, in the complex of relations which makes for bitterness and hatred in present-day Germany. These can be solved only as our relations are lifted to the level of God's dealing with us.

These three Bible studies have now to be linked together under the *Kirchentag* theme of 'Reconciliation'. There are many ways of showing that all three studies are closely connected. One may consider the first as dealing with the son, the second with the father, and the third with the brother. Thus the whole family relationship of God and mankind is worked out.

Or one may look at the three studies as a triptych, with Luke 22—that is the study of the Last Supper—as the great centre panel, flanked on either side with the parable of the prodigal son and the parable of the unforgiving servant.

Or one may take the three themes in order as: God has reconciled us; let us be reconciled to God; reconciliation with one another. Or it may be reconciliation, the reconciled, the reconcilers.

Or analysing it in another way under the heading of reconciliation, the three great components are considered in these studies: sin, love, forgiveness. While all three are in all the studies, they are emphasized in this order in the three examples of reconciliation.

Every man who conducts Bible study will link the three in a different way, but it is important to see that they come in this order, and that there is a developing theme. It is only in this way that the *Kirchentag* can be prevented from becoming a semi-political discussion, saying the things that everybody wants to hear. The purpose of these Bible studies is quite different: it is to hear what God will say to his people in their present-day situation.

'Take and Read'

These notes on four Bible passages are designed to help members of the churches in Yeovil prepare for their Bible Week. The passages have been chosen because of their Advent theme and they have already been the subject of discussion by the ministers of the town. They will be the subject of many sermons in the pulpits of Yeovil on Sunday 7 December, which is the opening of Bible Week. On the four successive evenings each of the passages will be expounded in the Parish Church to a united congregation. Before then it will be necessary for those who are going to take part in the Week to prepare themselves by reading the passages and studying them, preferably in group Bible study. The notes are based upon the discussion which the ministers have had together and they have worked on the principle that the Bible speaks to Yeovil today. Most of the passages are parables. They are a report of what Jesus said when he was with the disciples. They were written down a generation or so later by followers of Jesus who thought that they still had importance in the very different circumstances of their lives. There are many things which Jesus said which were not preserved, and presumably these were chosen because of their special importance and because they continued to be relevant to a later generation. It is not surprising therefore that we should expect them to be relevant to our generation. We have worked on the assumption that God has something to say to the people of Yeovil through these passages.

It is your task as you prepare for Bible Week to read the passages, and to discover what God is saying to you. The notes are intended to help you do that.

I. *The Parables of the Kingdom. Matthew* 13. 24-52.

There are several parables in this section, and they are carefully arranged to bring out certain aspects of the teaching of Jesus. Embedded in them is also an explanation of one of the parables as well as a description of what a parable really is.

First look at the shape of the passage and see what it contains. It is balanced like a picture. If you arrange the parables in parallel columns, you can see that each has its counterpart and each adds a little to the meaning of the other. This is how the parables are arranged:

Wheat and Tares	The Drag-net
vv. 24-30	vv. 47-50
Mustard Seed	Leaven
vv. 31-32	v. 33
Hidden Treasure	Pearl
v. 44	vv. 45-46

All these six parables are described as telling us something about the kingdom of heaven. We must not be too concerned about the grammatical structure of the verses when they say, 'The kingdom of heaven is like . . .' The thing which follows such a comparison is really the whole parable and not some one element in it. For example, in v. 24 the kingdom of heaven is not to be compared to a man. All that the phrase means is that the parable will light up our understanding of the kingdom of heaven. Before we come to these pairs of parables and their different meanings, it may be as well to look at what we are told in the passage about the purpose of parables, and the example that we are given in vv. 36-43 about the way to understand a parable.

The purpose of parables is described twice in chapter 13 but we have only one of these explanations in our passage; it is vv. 34-35. There is a much more difficult explanation given earlier in the chapter which you may like to refer back to and discuss. In vv. 34-35 we are told that Jesus always spoke in parables and the reason for this is given in a quotation from Ps. 78. If you read that Psalm, you will see it is about God's intention to reveal things which have not been known before. The quotation from the Psalm becomes not only an exact quotation of two lines, but a summary of the Psalm itself:

> I will open my mouth in parables;
> I will utter what has been hidden from
> the foundation of the world.

The parable is then a special way of thinking that will make something clear that has been hidden. It is, as we discover, a method of telling something that can be interpreted in many different ways. A parable is not easy, and, as we see in v. 36, even the disciples did not always understand them. Yet the parable is never intended to obscure, it is intended to make clear. That is the first point that needs careful study and discussion. The parable reveals something, therefore we must ask, 'How are we to explain a parable?' In this section we have one example. The disciples come to Jesus and ask him what the parable of the tares and the wheat really means. He goes through the parable step by step, patiently explaining what each part means, almost like someone who is explaining in words of one syllable a joke that he has made. There is nothing so deflating as having to explain a story which ought to have been evident at the first hearing. One may perhaps detect a trace of impatience in Jesus as he is explaining these details to the disciples—it nearly destroys the parable. Yet it does say something about the parable and gives us teaching which is of great value. We shall come back to this passage, but for the moment let us see in it one way of interpreting the parable. It is not the only way, or Jesus would have given that explanation also to the crowd. The parable is always a vivid story. It is drawn from experiences that the crowd can understand. Some of our difficulties with the parables are not difficulties of understanding the teaching, but of relating the everyday experiences of first-century Palestine to everyday experiences of twentieth-century Yeovil. Some of the experiences common to the first hearers are not common experiences to us. Our first attempt therefore in looking at the parable should be to recover the clarity of a real story. If the story itself seems strange, we are likely to miss the point of the parable. These are all good stories that Jesus told, and we have to remove the dust of centuries and share in their freshness.

When we have recovered the freshness of the parable, the point may become obvious. If not, it will be well to look in the New Testament to see if any hints are given to help us understand the parable. These hints do not take the place of the parable, but they generally show its main emphasis. They are rather like the frame which surrounds a picture—important, but no part of the picture itself. Then, finally, we have to ask ourselves what this parable means for us today. We shall try to do these things with all the parables in this section.

The Wheat and the Tares. vv. 24-30

When Jesus told this story it was almost certainly longer than it is in these verses. When we read it it helps to imagine some of the details and see how it could be filled

out. For example, there must have been a point of reference
—there was probably a field at hand where weeds were
growing among the wheat, and the natural comment of any
passer-by would be 'Bad farming!' If anyone wanted to
challenge that remark, he could well say to the man who
had made it, 'Well, what would you do if you woke up
one morning and found that your field which you thought
was of wheat, included tares?' That could be a perfectly
reasonable beginning to the story of a man who was a good
farmer, and who had taken care to prepare his ground and
choose the best seed. Jesus told such a story. Even the summary that we have in this passage uses words that give the
sense of progress in the story. The man sows good seed in
his field. While the men are sleeping his enemy comes and
sows other seed beside it. Verse 25 uses special words to
show both the action of the enemy and the kind of seed
that he sows. He is not simply described as sowing bad
seed—he sows a special kind of weed which will later
poison the wheat, and the verb used suggests almost that he
puts every seed beside another seed. He thoroughly mixes
up his sowing with the sowing of 'the men'. The words give
a sense of secrecy about this whole act which is suddenly
revealed when both the wheat and the tares grow up together. Then it is that the farmer's servants come to him
and ask him what they should do. They have recognized
the mixed harvest that will come, and they know the danger of that. The master has then to take a decision. He decides to let the two grow together until the harvest. It is
at this point that the hearers are asked to make their decision. In almost every parable, Jesus requires his hearers
to make a decision. It may come at the end or in the middle,
but it is nearly always there. The question now is, 'What

would you have done? Would you have weeded the field, or would you have left it and done the weeding at harvest time?' It is because of that point of decision that we can imagine a real field with a mixed crop of weeds and wheat providing the occasion for a parable. Jesus often refers to something which his hearers can see. Now he goes on and says that this man decided to leave the crop because it would have been difficult to pull up the weeds without disturbing the wheat. At harvest time the distinction is clear enough. He is accepting the danger which would come with a careless harvesting. If any of the weeds were harvested in with the wheat they would poison it. There is a perfectly good story which any hearer of his day would have recognized as a real case for decision and as a possible story. Enemies sometimes did sow tares among the wheat. But what was Jesus saying through this parable? He left it in their minds, something they were not likely to forget. Whatever meaning they got from it at once would not be the only meaning this story would give them. As you read it through again, try to see what possible meaning it could have as you listen to it as a story supposed to throw light on your understanding of the kingdom of heaven. It is inevitable that your mind should be fixed on one or other of the two high points in the story : the time of decision, when the master has either to leave the field or weed it; and the time of harvest, when a real separation has to be made. Both these points are in the parable as it was first told. We have the impression of patience and of separation. We must decide how they throw light on the kingdom of heaven. The more you try to understand the parable, the more you sympathize with the disciples who could understand the story well enough but who just couldn't see the point.

The Explanation. vv. 36-43

As Jesus seeks to answer their question, you can imagine
him saying, 'One way of understanding this story is to look
at it piece by piece.' He then casts a frame round the picture. The man who sows the good seed is compared to him;
the field is the world; the good seed is called the children
of the kingdom—that is first of all the disciples; the tares
are compared to those other people who are mixed up in
the kingdom with his disciples, planted there not by himself but by the enemy. The enemy then you can think of
as the devil. So far, if you think of the parable in this way,
the first decision in the parable has to be made by Jesus
himself. He is the Lord of the Church, and here he is described as being patient and tolerant with the very mixed
character of his Church. Indeed we can remember that even
his disciples were very mixed. Judas was among them, and
he left him there as one of the Twelve. He did not attempt
to root out the weeds at an early stage. But he goes on in
this explanation to compare the harvest to the end of the
world. Neither in the parable itself nor in this explanation
can we escape the purpose of telling the parable as a description of the kingdom as something which is to come at
the end of time. So we have in the parable two lights on the
kingdom. One is that it is pressing in on us now and includes very different kinds of people; the other is that at
some stage there has to be a separation. This explanation
given by Jesus needs to be read carefully. It is not the only
explanation of the parable, but it is one. We need to hold
the vivid picture of this parable in our minds, let the light
of his explanation fall upon it and then hear what God is
saying to us through it. At the end of v. 43 this is put briefly
'He who has ears, let him hear'—or as J. B. Phillips trans-

lates this, 'Let those who have ears use them.' There seem to be three things said which have importance for all periods, including our own.

  (1) Evil is no part of God's will.
  (2) Evil is intertwined with good.
  (3) Evil cannot be tolerated at the last.

The Drag-net. vv. 47-50

This is a brief parable saying much the same things as the parable of the wheat and the tares. The drag-net is a net which scours the bottom of the sea and brings in all kinds of things. Good and bad are heaped up together in the net, and not until it has been dragged to the shore can there be any separation. It would be well to read this parable in the light of what you have learned from the first. The two parables should be compared.

The Mustard Seed and the Leaven. vv. 31-33

These two short parables mean much the same thing. They are vivid pictures of a growth which is unsuspected. A tiny mustard seed can hardly be expected to grow into a huge herb, almost a tree. A tiny piece of leaven lost in the mass of dough can hardly be expected to transform the whole mass. Both pictures are taken from everyday life, and both are such as might have been given as a result of observation or a question. The parable of the leaven would have special meaning for a Jewish audience, because the rabbis taught that leaven indicated something evil. Unleavened bread was considered to be good, but when it was leavened some kind of evil was put into it. The Jew would not eat that leavened bread. The parable could then become much more alive if we saw it as a side reference to the liking that some Jews had for leavened bread. The woman is described as hiding the leaven in the lump—this may be no more than showing how small the leaven is, but it could also suggest a kind of surreptitious putting in of the leaven when nobody was looking. So the second parable does add something to the first. Both tell of slow and inevitable growth from something small to something unexpectedly big. The second one goes further and shows that this thing cannot be hidden—you cannot hide your leaven in the dough any more than this woman could. Eventually it leavens the whole lump and the neighbours can see that she has leavened bread. These few verses should now be read carefully and pictured. They are not very far from our everyday experience. We have all seen examples of small seeds which have grown into large trees—the acorn becomes an oak tree. Many have seen the action of yeast at work in a bakery and know how small a piece of yeast can influence a large amount of dough. What light do these two pictures throw on the kingdom of heaven?

The Hidden Treasure and the Pearl. vv. 44-46

Again these two parables teach much the same thing. We are not asked to judge of the honesty of the man who bought a field knowing that there was a treasure in it, or of the wisdom of the merchant who sells all his merchandise and buys one pearl. We are simply given vivid pictures of decisions that some men take. If you had the chance of buying a field in which you knew a valuable treasure was hidden, then you might sell everything you had in order to buy the field. To outsiders who know nothing of what the field contains, it looks like a stupid action. Much the same can be said of the merchant and the pearl. Outsiders who know nothing of the value of the pearl that he is buying will think him foolish to get rid of so much in order to buy one pearl. The pictures are clearly throwing light upon the kingdom of heaven and what a man willingly gives up in order to enter it. This is a call to discipleship. The verses should be read carefully to see what light they throw on our understanding of the Christian life. Many examples can be given from your own experience of self-denial which seems to be foolish.

As you read the whole passage through again there are certain questions that should be asked. The kingdom of heaven cannot be identified with the Church, but to a certain extent we can think of these parables as throwing light upon the Church also.

(1) How far should a Christian separate himself from the world? and how far should he 'grow up together with it until the harvest'?

(2) Is the growth of the Church inevitable or does it depend upon our activities?

(3) How far is a man prepared to go in self-denial and can his self-denial buy him a way into the Church?

This material enabled groups to meet together and discuss what the parables meant to Yeovil. The initial thinking had been done, but each group had to follow through with real application—and then obey.

A BIBLE STUDY GROUP

The Book of Hosea had been chosen as a study book before the group realized how difficult it was. They had thought it a good idea to take an Old Testament book, and turned naturally to the twelve small books at the end of the Old Testament. These minor prophets seemed to offer material that could be dealt with in a few weeks. The study of Isaiah, some of them said, would take a lifetime. So they began with the first of the minor prophets, Hosea. No study outline had been prepared, but a leader agreed to come and explain to them when necessary the Hebrew background to the book. They had taken their way through the first chapter, using the Authorized Version, with a good deal of explanation from the leader about why children were called such strange names, and then they launched upon the long poetic section of chapter 2. The following is an attempt to reconstruct what was said.

Leader: In the first chapter we had the strange setting of the Book of Hosea, with Hosea marrying a prostitute, and calling his children by strange names. You'll remember the names were Jezreel, which was in the good tradition of the prophets—this meant that judgment would come upon the house of Jehu; then the next two had strange names that indicated that God was going to give up Israel. First, Loruhamah, which means 'I will not have mercy'—the 'Lo' was the negative; then Lo-ammi, which means 'You are not my people'. Now chapter 2 starts, apparently, with an address to Jezreel by his father Hosea.

> 'Say ye unto your brethren, Ammi; and to
> your sisters, Ruhamah.'

Hosea says, 'Call your brethren, and call them not by their proper names but by the names of "Ammi" and "Ruhamah" '. That is his way of saying—by dropping the negative—that God is recognizing Israel as his people again and that he will have mercy on them. It may seem to us an odd way to do it, but that is the way the prophets behaved. Instead of preaching sermons they did things. Hosea was drastic enough to get married, and here he is putting into the mouth of his children the thing that he wants to say to the people of Israel.

Member of group: Yes, but he's saying something quite different from what he said last week, except that the end of chapter 1 seems to run right into this verse. Isn't it really a continuation of chapter 1, then?

Leader: Yes, it is that, but there has been a change of message, and we must see several years, I think, between v. 9 in chapter 1 and v. 10. Really I think chapter 2 ought to begin with 1. 10, which is where it does begin in the Hebrew. Some years afterwards, God is saying that he will yet avenge the blood of Jezreel in favour of Israel and not against her.

First member: Then who is speaking in 2. 1, if it continues there?

Second member: Well, I think it's Hosea, although it could be God; it would be a more natural continuation from chapter 1. If it is Hosea speaking, then he is calling his oldest boy, Jezreel, and asking him to call his brother and his sister by these changed names. If it is God speaking, then he is telling Hosea that he must in the presence of his brethren call his children by these changed names.

First member: There's a lot of talk of vengeance in this book—won't that lead us to think that we have the right to go and avenge?

Third member: Yes, I think that is one of the dangers of reading the Old Testament, and one reason why some people dismiss it as pagan. But it is only the first chapter so far, and while the book continues to talk a bit about vengeance, the real message of this second chapter is that God does not avenge. Isn't there a verse that reserves vengeance for God and not for man, anyway?

First member: Yes, 'Vengeance is mine, saith the Lord, I will repay.'

Second member: Then is there a difference? Has God the right to avenge and men not?

First member: God has lots of things that we don't have and we have to get on without them. I don't always see why he should have them and we not, but it seems to be a fact.

Third member: One of the things he has of course is a completely clear vision. When he avenges he does not make a mistake. Although I'm not agreeing that vengeance is a good thing, what makes it an even worse thing is the possibility that we may be wrong.

Leader: There are many stories of vengeance where an innocent man has been killed mistakenly. But the message of this second chapter is that God, having the right to avenge, is not going to use it. Hosea learns this, and I think it would be a good thing if we could read the next passage, vv. 2-7.

Fourth member: Plead with your mother, plead: for she is not my wife, neither am I her husband: let her therefore put away her whoredoms out of her sight, and her adulteries from between her breasts;

3. Lest I strip her naked, and set her as in the day that she was born, and make her as a wilderness, and set her like a dry land, and slay her with thirst.

4. And I will not have mercy upon her children; for they be the children of whoredoms.

5. For their mother hath played the harlot: she that conceived them hath done shamefully: for she said, I will go after my lovers, that give me my bread and my water, my wool and my flax, mine oil and my drink.

6. Therefore, behold, I will hedge up thy way with thorns, and make a wall, that she shall not find her paths.

7. And she shall follow after her lovers, but she shall not overtake them; and she shall seek them, but shall not find them : then shall she say, I will go and return to my first husband; for then was it better with me than now.

Leader: In this passage Hosea is thoroughly mixing up his relation with his wife and God's relation with Israel. Some of the phrases apply to his own domestic problems; the others apply to God's dealings with Israel. In fact, the prophet is learning about God and what God feels from his own experiences.

First member: He says in v. 4, 'And I will not have mercy upon her children'—well, it isn't their fault.

Second member: What part do the children play in all this? Is Hosea thinking now of his domestic situation or is he thinking of Israel?

First member: Well, if you believe in a God of mercy, the only way you can understand this passage is to take it as referring to the children of Israel—they would be responsible for their errors but the children of Gomer cannot be blamed for being hers.

Leader: I think you will find in the Old Testament a much greater sense of solidarity of the family than we have today. When one member of a family does anything wrong, the whole family is counted as guilty. We are much more individualistic than they were, you know.

First member: Well, I think in many ways that's a good thing.

Third member: Yes, I think it is, and it helps us to understand the prophets better if we will realize that the family is very closely linked together. But it raises problems, because you constantly get these phrases like 'the sins of the father shall be visited upon the children to the third and fourth generation'. And you get these dreadful Psalms which talk about dashing children to pieces. I don't think we can agree entirely with this solidarity—the sense of the individual is something which we have learnt. And it is something which is learnt already in the pages of the Old Testament. Can you remember the point at which it is learnt?

First member: Oh yes, didn't Jeremiah object to the old saying, 'The fathers have eaten sour grapes and the children's teeth are set on edge'?

Leader: Yes, Ezekiel did too. It was later than Hosea, though, that these prophets discovered the importance of the individual and that every man should be responsible for his own wrong-doing and not for somebody else's.

First member: But it isn't as simple as all that. We are related to each other and we are responsible for the wrong-doings of other people. We can't just do as we please and we can't do wrong without hurting somebody else. It is all bound up together and I think Hosea's right in some ways.

Leader: Well that takes us back to Hosea anyway. As I see these verses they are comparing God's dealing with Israel to Hosea's dealing with his wife. The story seems fairly simple: his wife has gone out after other men and has been attracted by their presents. She has forgotten that her husband has really given her far more than they have. She has chosen now to leave her husband and go in search of those who have given her gifts. Now Hosea in his sorrow asks himself what he will do, and as he thinks about what he should do he realizes that the situation is just like God's dealing with Israel. God had given to Israel everything, brought her out of slavery into the promised land. There she had discovered other gods and liked them, and now she was leaving God and looking for her other gods. Hosea thinks of preventing her from finding her lovers and bringing home to her the fact that she owes far more to her husband than she realizes, so that she will come back to him, and he sees that God is doing just the same to Israel. I think as we go on in this chapter we shall have to recognize these two strands sometimes getting thoroughly mixed, of Hosea and his wife, God and Israel.

First member: She presumably left her husband because she found him dull!

Leader: Yes, that may be true. And it also is a parallel with God and Israel because Israel found the worship of God rather dull too. You get many hints throughout the Bible that there was much more excitement and a good deal more sensual pleasure in worshipping the gods of the land than there was in the pure worship of the God of Israel.

First member: Well, how far do you think we should go in our own efforts to make worship now more interesting?

Leader: That is something which each church must decide for itself, but clearly you can't go as far as these Canaanite religions.

Third member: Yet there is something in that question. You can see it in some Latin-American countries, particularly, where the worship of the traditional Protestant churches does seem dull compared with the Catholic worship from which the people have come, or the Pentecostal worship to which the crowds flock.

Leader: This is getting away from Hosea and is not really a true parallel. What this passage says is that these gods of Canaan really do not care for Israel any more than these lovers of Gomer really care for her. When they have what they want then they leave her. The judgment of Israel is coming. Hosea has in fact seen clearly that Israel is going to be destroyed. In the moment of that destruction, who will care for her? Certainly not the Canaanite gods. In that day she will have to return to God. Then she will realize who it was who gave her the things that she most desired. But that is anticipating the chapter. We'd better read the next section, vv. 8-13.

Fifth member: For she did not know that I gave her corn, and wine, and oil, and multiplied her silver and gold, which they prepared for Baal.
9. Therefore will I return, and take away my corn in the time thereof, and my wine in the season thereof, and will recover my wool and my flax given to cover her nakedness.
10. And now will I discover her lewdness in the sight of her lovers, and none shall deliver her out of mine hand.
11. I will also cause all her mirth to cease, her feast days, her new moons, and her sabbaths, and all her solemn feasts.
12. And I will destroy her vines and her fig trees, whereof she hath said, These are my rewards that my lovers have given me: and I will make them a forest, and the beasts of the field shall eat them.
13. And I will visit upon her the days of Baalim, wherein she burned incense to them, and she decked herself with her earrings and her jewels, and she went after her lovers, and forgat me, saith the Lord.

First member: Does it really mean in v. 8 that 'she did not *know* that I gave her . . .'?
Leader: It depends upon who is asking the question. If it is Israel, then it is perfectly clear. Most of the Canaanite gods were fertility and agricultural gods. The Israelites who had turned away from their God and worshipped other gods presumably really believed that by this worship they got

great harvests. I suppose it's also possible that that could partly apply to Gomer—she had taken for granted what she got at home. But we must not press the parallel too far. Hosea has thoroughly muddled the two relations because he himself is learning one from the other. He may see that what he wants to do with Gomer is to prove to her that if he took away his support entirely then she would be in a bad state. This may not be a modern way for a husband to deal with an erring wife, but it's fairly typical of the period.

Third member: What does v. 9 mean when he speaks of 'take away my corn in the time thereof'? What is the time thereof?

Second member: That means the harvest. They will have a bad harvest.

Third member: Then this must be referring to Israel?

Leader: Oh yes. Although v. 9 could with a little stretch be made to apply to Gomer also, because presumably he made her an allowance of corn and wine.

Third member: And it could apply to her if it meant that Hosea just didn't give her an allowance; and certainly the second part of the verse applies more to her than to the land, perhaps.

First member: Oh, but 'nakedness' could apply to a land without a harvest just as much as to a person.

Fourth member: Do you think this passage has any meaning for us in God's dealing with us?

First member: I hope not!

Fourth member: It does mean that when we forget how much we depend upon God we sometimes need a reminder. Would it not be a good thing if God withdrew his gifts for a while? I think sometimes in years of bad harvests we are more inclined to remember God than in years of good harvests.

First member: I don't know. Take the example of the weather. When you have a bad summer you don't remember to be grateful for the good ones you have had—you simply remember them and feel sorry for yourself now.

Second member: The weather is not quite the same as the harvest, unless you happen to be a farmer whose crop depends upon the weather. The only time when the weather seems to me to bring us back sharply to a remembrance of God is when we have a severe drought and then the churches are asked to pray for rain.

Third member: I think if you lived in the country and saw how much your prosperity depends upon the harvest, you would be much more inclined to think of God when your harvest is in danger. When it's a good harvest you are inclined to take it for granted.

Leader: So far we have had Hosea wanting to stop her going to her lovers and then taking away from her his support so that she realizes how much she depends upon him. This is compared to God's concern for Israel. Both actions are intended to bring her back. Now we get the gentle side of Hosea's character. Someone had better read vv. 14-18.

Fifth member: Therefore, behold, I will allure her, and bring her into the wilderness, and speak comfortably unto her.

15. And I will give her her vineyards from thence, and the valley of Achor for a door of hope: and she shall sing there, as in the days of her youth, and as in the day when she came up out of the land of Egypt.

16. And it shall be at that day, saith the Lord, that thou shalt call me Ishi; and shalt call me no more Baali.

17. For I will take away the names of Baalim out of her mouth, and they shall no more be remembered by their name.

18. And in that day will I make a covenant for them with

the beasts of the field, and with the fowls of heaven, and with the creeping things of the ground: and I will break the bow and the sword and the battle out of the earth, and will make them to lie down safely.

Leader: There again you have the two mixed up Hosea's ideal is to take Gomer back to the days of her youth and to woo her again as a young man woos his sweetheart. The parallel to that in God's dealing with Israel is to go back to the day when he brought her out of the land of Egypt, to the day when they were in the wilderness coming towards the promised land, before she had ever met the Canaanite gods. The two words 'Ishi' and 'Baali' here in v. 16 represent two different relationships. One is 'My man' and the other is 'My master'. This is the difference of the relationship between husband and wife, and the relationship between master and slave. Hosea would teach Gomer to be a wife again and God wants to teach Israel to be in a covenant relation with him and not a race of slaves.

First member: She doesn't have to do anything about going back; he comes and looks for her.

Second member: Yes, this is about as near as we get to the parable of the lost sheep. Yet she does have to do something. She has to accept her position as his wife.

First member: That's not very easy.

Leader: Who for?

Third member: For either of them.

Leader: I'm quite sure Hosea realizes that in his own personal life, and is beginning to see that it is also true in God's relation with Israel. This is really the strength of Hosea's prophecy. He is learning about relations in his own personal life and, as the result of that, discovering the true relation between God and Israel.

Third member: This is really a quite remarkable thing for eight centuries before Christ. God does not want to be simply the master of Israel. He wants to be to her as a husband.
Leader: It is this discovery in Hosea which has made so many people think of this prophet as the one who first understood the meaning of the Cross.

The last few verses of this chapter pretty well sum it up.

Fourth member: And I will betroth thee unto me for ever; yea, I will betroth thee unto me in righteousness, and in judgment, and in lovingkindness, and in mercies.
20. I will even betroth thee unto me in faithfulness: and thou shalt know the Lord.
21. And it shall come to pass in that day, I will hear, saith the Lord, I will hear the heavens, and they shall hear the earth;
22. and the earth shall hear the corn, and the wine, and the oil; and they shall hear Jezreel.
23. And I will sow her unto me in the earth; and I will have mercy upon her that had not obtained mercy; and I will say to them which were not my people, Thou art my people; and they shall say, Thou art my God.

Second member: That's a beautiful picture.
Leader: That seems complete in itself, but we shall see when we come to chapter 3 that there is a great deal more to be done. Hosea is sent out to buy back Gomer because by now she has become a slave, being sold in the marketplace. But that belongs to chapter 3.

So far we have followed the discussion of the meaning of the passage. Now, the application of this passage to daily life is possible, as it would not have been to many members of the group before. They all now have enough knowledge to discuss on an equal level. Leader and group search together.

4

CHOOSING A BOOK TO STUDY

ANY group faced with the whole Bible might cast around for help before choosing a book to study. There are many denominational helps, and syllabuses have been prepared to see that Bible study groups cover the more important parts of the Bible. There are those that have been designed to take groups progressively through more and more difficult passages; there are syllabuses planned quite mechanically to make sure that a group misses nothing of the Bible; there are syllabuses planned doctrinally so that the major doctrines of the Christian faith can be considered in turn and in a certain logical order. All these have their place, but any one group, or for that matter an individual, might not wish to follow a long course of training. There may be uncertainty as to whether the group is going to have a long life at all. It may have been a group that has come together quite haphazardly, and it may even be an interdenominational group. It may be a group with a certain independent turn of mind that wants to choose its own book.

There may be many reasons why a group needs some guidance in choosing the book on which to start. It will be wise if it takes some time to decide, because the choice of the wrong book may put a group off for ever. I know a group which started on the Book of Daniel. They had a good beginning, because the early chapters of Daniel contain some excellent stories and examples of courage which can be discussed. For the first half of the book they managed quite well and, although some of the visions were a bit strange to them, they were able, with the help of commentaries, to make their way through the early chapters. But before long they had got lost in the prophecies, and in sheer weariness they gave up Bible study altogether. It took a long time to convince that group that Bible study was worth doing and was exciting. If they had had proper outlines or study notes they might even have got through the Book of Daniel, but in any case it was not a good book with which to begin.

The group should know roughly what it is choosing when it decides upon a book. That means taking the trouble to find out what the books are about and what one can expect from studying them. The Bible is after all a collection of books and not just one single book to be gone through from beginning to end. The worst possible way for a group to study the Bible is to begin at the beginning and go through to the end. I defy any group to get through the Book of Numbers or even Leviticus with real interest.

The books of the Bible are very different in kind. In the New Testament most people know that they have four versions of the ministry of Jesus. The Gospels are fairly well known. Then there is the account of the early Christian Church in the Acts of the Apostles, followed by a number of letters, and then finally the book of the Revelation, which groups should keep off until they have been going a long time. The letters represent a strange collection, and they may be tempting to a group because some of them are so short.

Choosing a book to study

There is a lot to be said for choosing a short book, because the study can then be over before interest in that book has flagged. Many of these letters are by the Apostle Paul, and they can be studied much better if they are related to events in the life of Paul as they are described in the Acts of the Apostles. There is a great deal to be said for beginning a Bible study group with one of the earliest of Paul's letters, that to the Galatians. It has practically everything that a good Bible study group needs. It has narrative at the beginning which can be compared with the account of the same incidents in the Acts of the Apostles; it has two chapters of good doctrinal teaching which are written with vigour and contain some of the best verses in the Bible; it has also some practical instructions at the end of the letter which can be compared with Christian ethics today. When a group sits down to study the Epistle to the Galatians it knows roughly what it is going to meet and then it can plunge in and make discoveries.

It is as well before starting any book to find out what it is all about. The Epistles to the Thessalonians, for example, are likely to be too difficult and involved, requiring a great deal more background material than the average group possesses. There are many books written giving summaries of the books of the Bible, and it would be useful for a group, before deciding upon which book it is going to study, to go through one of these summaries and make its choice according to the content. Fairly early a group should study one of the Gospels, and Luke is as good as any to start with. It contains some of the birth stories, it has some of the best parables, and it is told in a style which is a little less strange to us than Matthew.

But the Old Testament should not be neglected and

neither should it be left until the New Testament is finished.
I would suggest that after a Gospel, perhaps the Acts of
the Apostles and one of the letters of the New Testament
have been studied, the group should get on as quickly as
possible to a book of the Old Testament. It is probably best
to go to the prophets, but it is as well to know straightaway
what the Old Testament contains.

The first five books are what the Jews call the Torah, that
is the Law, but you will soon discover that the Law does
not simply mean a list of laws. These five books contain
some of the best stories in the Bible. Then follow the historical books, from Joshua to Nehemiah. A group could
have a good short series of studies on the Book of Ruth.
Esther is a rather strange book, not mentioning the word
'God' once, and yet telling of God's dealings with an under-
privileged people. Esther is a story rather than a book for
study.

Job is quite different. With a good leader the Book of
Job can be studied with great profit. One valuable procedure
here is to begin by studying the setting of the Book of Job,
that is, the way in which the problem is posed in the pro-
logue and the epilogue, then take the central poem as a
whole and study the speeches of Job, omitting the speeches
of his friends for the time being. That gives chapter by
chapter the spiritual progress of a man who is being
tempted and who is suffering. For such a book a group does
need a good leader, but it can be one of the most profitable
books in the Bible.

After that few of the poetical books of the Bible—Psalms,
Proverbs, Ecclesiastes, the Song of Solomon—make good
study books.

The Prophets are left to us, and if we put to one side the

very long ones, we have the twelve minor prophets from Hosea to Malachi. One of these twelve makes a good choice for a beginning. Hosea is difficult but interesting; Amos will give a good opportunity for discussing social problems; Jonah is perhaps the best of the twelve with which to begin.

The Book of Jonah has an immediate interest because everybody has heard of Jonah and the whale. That is a misplaced emphasis and a group can do a great deal to correct the mistake. The first thing that needs to be seen is that the Book of Jonah is the story of a reluctant missionary. Once the 'Jonah and the Whale' incident has been put into its proper setting, the Book of Jonah is an excellent book for careful study by a group, and will certainly be found to speak to this generation.

Another book of great value for a group is the Book of the prophet Haggai. This book can be studied quickly, probably in two or three sessions. It is better done so because of the speed with which the actions take place. The book should always be studied with a careful note of the dates of the events; the whole thing is over in a few months.

In this book I do not want to draw up a syllabus for anybody. That has been done again and again, and will be done by those whose job it is to see that their denomination is making a proper study of the Word of God. I have simply tried to indicate how a book can be chosen for study, and I would emphasize the necessity of including in any syllabus a study of the Old Testament as well as the New.

SELECTED BOOKS FOR FURTHER GUIDANCE

Introduction to the Bible, Balmer H. Kelly, editor. Volume I, The Layman's Bible Commentary. Richmond: John Knox Press, 1959.

The Bible Speaks, Robert Davidson. New York: Thomas Y. Crowell Company, 1959.

Harper's Bible Dictionary, Madeleine S. and J. Lane Miller. New York: Harper and Brothers, 1955.

The Westminster Historical Atlas to the Bible, G. Ernest Wright and Floyd V. Filson, editors. Philadelphia: The Westminster Press, revised edition, 1956.

A Companion to the Bible, J. J. van Allmen, editor. New York: Oxford University Press, 1958.

A Handbook of Christian Theology, New York: Meridian Books, 1958.

Dietrich Bonhoeffer, *The Cost of Discipleship*, new complete ed., Macmillan, 1959.

C. S. Lewis, *Reflections on the Psalms*, Harcourt, 1958.

William Neil, *The Rediscovery of the Bible*, Harper, 1954.

D. T. Niles, *Reading the Bible Today* (World Christian Books), Association Press, 1955.

INDEX OF BIBLICAL PASSAGES DISCUSSED